Sir Ernest Shackleton

LINDA DAVIS

GREAT EXPLORERS

Sir Ernest Shackleton

LINDA DAVIS

CHELSEA HOUSE
PUBLISHERS
An imprint of Infobase Publishing

GREAT EXPLORERS: SIR ERNEST SHACKLETON

Chelsea House
An imprint of Infobase Publishing
132 West 31st Street
New York NY 10001

Library of Congress Cataloging-in-Publication Data
Davis, Linda, 1973-
  Sir Ernest Shackleton / Linda Davis.
     p. cm. — (Great explorers)
  Includes bibliographical references and index.
  ISBN 978-1-60413-421-6 (hardcover)
  1. Shackleton, Ernest Henry, Sir, 1874-1922—Juvenile literature. 2. Explorers
—Great Britain—Biography—Juvenile literature. 3. Antarctica—Discovery
and exploration—British—Juvenile literature. I. Title. II. Series.
  G875.S5D38 2009
  919.8'9—dc22
  [B]   2009014164

Chelsea House books are available at special discounts when purchased in bulk quantities for businesses, associations, institutions, or sales promotions. Please call our Special Sales Department in New York at (212) 967-8800 or (800) 322-8755.

You can find Chelsea House on the World Wide Web at
http://www.chelseahouse.com

Series design by Lina Farinella
Cover design by Keith Trego

Printed in the United States of America

Bang EJB 10 9 8 7 6 5 4 3 2 1

This book is printed on acid-free paper.

All links and Web addresses were checked and verified to be correct at the time of publication. Because of the dynamic nature of the Web, some addresses and links may have changed since publication and may no longer be valid.

CONTENTS

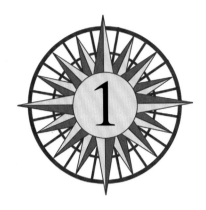

Stranded!

AT 5 O'CLOCK IN THE EVENING, ERNEST SHACKLETON GAVE the order to abandon ship. No one was surprised. For nearly nine months, the *Endurance* had been at the mercy of the ice—frozen motionless in the middle of the Weddell Sea. Those on board had hoped to be part of a great Trans-Antarctic Expedition. Now, they only hoped to make it back home. It would not be aboard the ship that carried them there: the *Endurance*. The ice around the ship was pushing together, trying with all its might to expel the foreign object trapped within its surface.

Earlier in the day, most of the forecastle beams had already split. The deck was buckled, heaving up and down with the pressure like the chest of a living beast. Frank Wild—the second in command—made his way throughout the ship. He stuck his head inside the crew's quarters. "She's going boys," he said in a strangely calm tone. "I think it's time to get off." Wild walked to the propeller shaftway. There, McNeish, the ship's carpenter, and McLeod, a sailor, were busy stuffing torn pieces of blankets into a hole that had been punched out by the ice. But the water was ankle deep and rising. Nothing would hold it back now. Wild signaled for them to give it up.

The surface of the ice was moving. Jagged sheets of ice that looked as if they were pieced together like a jigsaw puzzle stretched as far as the eye could see. An invisible force was shoving them tightly together. Wherever two thick floes came together, the edges scraped and groaned for a time. Neither floe would yield to the other. Slowly, with a quiver, they would rise, tenting up until one or both of them broke and toppled over, creating a pressure ridge. The sounds of the moving pack haunted the men's sleeping and waking hours. There were cracks, moans, booms, and creaks at all hours.

By seven o'clock, the men had transferred all the essential gear to the ice. They were busy setting up camp on a solid floe a few hundred yards away from the ship. In the weeks that followed, they would come to know this place as Ocean Camp. Shackleton ordered a few men to go back to the ship to retrieve some other necessities. One of them was Alexander Macklin, a stocky young physician. The other was Wild. The men picked their way through the blocks of ice that had tumbled onto the forecastle. Then they carefully lifted the hatch and went below. The noise inside was horrific. The half-empty forepeak compartment served as a giant sounding box, amplifying each crack and snap of splintering timber. The sides of the ship were only a few feet away from them. They could hear the ice outside banging against the ship, trying to break its way through.

As their eyes adjusted to the darkness, the scene continued to grow more terrifying. Posts and beams were bending and splitting on every side. The space on either side of them continued to narrow. They made their way to the bulkhead, which was bulged outward as if it might burst at any moment. The two men worked with feverish speed, but Macklin was sure they would never make it out in time. Much to their relief, they made it out fine. Later, Macklin confided in his diary, "I do not

During an attempt to cross Antarctica by way of the South Pole, Sir Ernest Shackleton and his crew were forced to abandon ship and establish a camp on the inhospitable continent. Stranded with limited supplies, Shackleton and his men watched as shifting ice floes slowly crushed and sank their vessel, the *Endurance* (*in background*).

think I have ever had such a horrible sickening sensation of fear as I had whilst in the hold of that breaking ship."

In actuality, the ship would stay above the ice for another month. On November 21, 1915, however, the ice won the battle.

The fatal blows began on October 24, when a sort of sluggish shock wave moved through the ice pack, setting into motion a frenzy of rolling, tumbling destruction. The ice wriggled and badgered *Endurance* until it was pinned up against two floes—fore and aft on the starboard side and jabbed in the center on the other. The tormented ship sounded like it was crying out in agony. The next evening, the pressure increased again. The floe on the port side scraped against the ship. A band of emperor penguins gathered a short distance away and stared at the ship. Emperors were a common sight, but none of the men had ever seen such a large group before. After a moment, the penguins raised their heads and let out a weird, mournful cry. Nobody—not even the Antarctic veterans—had ever heard penguins make any other sound than their typical croaking noises. The sailors immediately stopped what they were doing. One of them turned to Macklin. "Do you hear that?" he asked, "We'll none of us get back to our homes again."

In the early morning of November 21, Shackleton stepped out of his tent. Out of the corner of his eye, he noticed the *Endurance* move. He spun around and saw the stack disappear behind a pile of ice. "She's going boys!" he shouted and dashed up to the lookout for a better view. Within minutes, all hands were out of the tents, scrambling to get a good look. The camp watched in complete silence as the ship rose 20 feet into the air, hung there for a moment, then slowly sank beneath the surface. Only a small, black gap of open water remained where the *Endurance* had been imprisoned in the ice for more than nine months. A minute later, the ice closed up, leaving no trace of a ship ever having been there. The men were stranded, hundreds of miles away from land, on a frozen, volatile sea.

As their commander, Shackleton felt a tremendous weight of responsibility rest on his shoulders. He was responsible for these 27 lives, marooned on a floating ice island. He vowed to see them safely home—every last one of them alive.

Hero

Shackleton's order to abandon ship signaled the beginning of the greatest Antarctic adventure of all time. This was his third expedition to the Antarctic and one of the most ambitious expeditions ever attempted. The goal of the Imperial Trans-Antarctic Expedition was to cross the Antarctic continent from west to east, passing through the South Pole. But fate had another expedition in mind for Ernest Shackleton. His mission would be the rescue of his crew of castaways, an endeavor he attacked with brute determination and ultimate perseverance. In the face of insurmountable adversity, Shackleton was a model of courage and strength. His leadership and devotion through utter hopelessness defined heroism.

Although not the most successful of polar explorers, Shackleton became famous for his unrivaled strength as a genuine leader and his undeniable capability in desperate situations. As one of his men once wrote, "For scientific leadership give me Scott; for swift and efficient travel, Amundsen; but when you are in a hopeless situation, when there seems no way out, get down on your knees and pray for Shackleton." Only a true hero could lead his crew over 850 miles of the South Atlantic's most turbulent seas to the closest outpost of civilization and live to tell the astonishing tale.

Ancient maps labeled Antarctica as Terra Australis Incognita—the unknown southern land. The harsh, dangerous weather of the southern ocean, particularly in the south Atlantic, was a key factor in the discovery of Antarctica. Time after time, sailors blown off course by a storm discovered new land. Often, this new land was farther south than any previously known. While attempting to navigate around Cape Horn (the southernmost point of South America) in 1619, Spanish explorers Bartolomé and Gonzalo Garcia de Nodal were blown off course. Because of this mistake, they discovered a tiny group of islands they named Islas Diego Ramirez. These isles would be the most southerly recorded land for another 156 years.

In the 1770s, Captain James Cook sailed in search of Antarctica. He navigated through dangerous waters and pack ice, but failed to sight the continent. Still, he was the first person ever to cross the Antarctic Circle and discovered what are now known as the South Sandwich Islands. He wrote, "The risk one runs in exploring a coast in these unknown and icy seas, is so great, that I can be bold enough to say that no man will ever venture farther than I have done, and the lands which may lie to the South will never be explored . . ." Although he was a bold explorer, Cook was incorrect. Men eventually did go farther, beginning with sealers in the early 1820s.

The British Royal Navy sent Edward Bransfield to determine if the new land that sealers had been discovering was part of a continent or a string of islands. Bransfield was also ordered to chart harbors, collect natural science specimens, and take weather and magnetic readings. On January 16, 1820, he sighted Livingston Island, and on January 22 he made a landing on King George Island, claiming it for Great Britain. Sailing southwest, he discovered Deception Island, Tower Island, and the Bransfield Strait. On January 30, he and his crew were the first men to lay eyes on the mountains of the Antarctic Peninsula, a place he called "Trinity Land." Bransfield continued his explorations until the middle of March 1820, discovering Gibbs, O'Brien, Elephant, Seal, and Clarence Islands and becoming the first person in history to sail into the Weddell Sea.

At the same time, Russian captain Thaddeus von Bellingshausen had crossed the Antarctic Circle just west of the Greenwich Meridian. Bellingshausen was prevented from going farther south by a massive continental ice shelf. This was the Finibul Ice Shelf—the first sighting of the continent of Antarctica.

The first recorded landing on the Antarctic continent took place on February 7, 1821. Crewmen on the American sealer *Cecilia*, under Captain John Davis, landed at Hughes Bay looking for seals. Another significant event in Antarctic exploration took place in 1821. One officer and 10 men from the British sealer *Lord Melville* were forced to spend the winter on King George Island after their ship was driven offshore by a storm and did not return. They were rescued the following summer.

Between 1839 and 1843, British explorer James Clark Ross sailed to Antarctica to find the elusive pole. He had already found the north magnetic pole in 1831, so it seemed fitting that he should search for the southern one. Ross left England in early October 1839 in command of two ships— *Erebus* and *Terror*. During his expedition, he discovered the Ross Sea, Victoria Land, and the volcanoes Mount Erebus and Mount Terror, named after the expedition vessels. They sailed for 250 miles (400 kilometers) along the edge of the low, flat-topped ice shelf today known as the Ross Ice Shelf. Next, he attempted to penetrate south at about 55 degrees west, and explored the eastern side of what is now known as James Ross Island, discovering and naming Snow Hill Island and Seymour Island. While sailing as far south as possible, Ross learned that the south magnetic pole lay inland, inaccessible by sea.

After Ross's voyages, there was a 50-year break in Antarctic exploration. The attentions of governments turned to the Arctic and the search for the Northwest Passage. On December 19, 1898, Carsten Borchgrevink commanded the first scientific expedition to spend a winter on the continent of Antarctica: the British Antarctic Expedition, 1898–1900. On February 18, 1899, Borchgrevink landed and established camp at Cape Adare. Borchgrevink, nine other men, and 75 dogs spent the winter carrying out survey trips and collecting samples and meteorological data. The expedition zoologist,

Accounts from earlier expeditions of icy conditions and a mysterious continent at the bottom of the world piqued a strong interest in exploring Antarctica. Soon, explorers were organizing crews and began sailing southward in a race to be the first to reach the South Pole, located on the continent of Antarctica. Ernest Shackleton (*above*) first traveled to Antarctica as a crewmember on the *Discovery* in 1901.

Nikolai Hanson, died and was the first person to be buried on the Antarctic mainland. On February 16, 1900, Borchgrevink and two others climbed the Ross Ice Shelf and sledged to a latitude of 78 degrees 50 minutes south, also shown as 78°50'S. (Latitude is the measure in degrees (°) ranging from 0° at the equator to 90° at the poles: 90°N for the North Pole and 90°S for the South Pole. The degree of the line of latitude is then divided into 60 minutes (') and each minute is divided into 60 seconds ("). These measurements can pinpoint a location on a map.) This was as far south as anyone had ever gone, and it marked the beginning of a race to the South Pole.

In August 1901, Robert Scott's first Antarctic expedition, the National Antarctic Expedition, left England aboard the ship *Discovery*. Scott hoped to lead some of his land party to the Geographic South Pole. One of the men on board hoped to be a part of that historic party. His name was Ernest Shackleton.

Teenager on the High Seas

On February 15, 1874, Letitia Shackleton gave birth to her second child, Ernest Henry Shackleton, at their family farm in Kilkea, county Kildare, Ireland. Ernest was the first son in a family that would eventually grow into 10 children—eight girls and two boys.

Dr. Henry Shackleton had married Henrietta Letitia Sophia Gavan, known as Letitia, just two years earlier. Henry had attended school at Wellington College in England, hoping to enlist in the army. Because of health problems, however, he was not accepted into the army and returned to Ireland to finish school at Trinity College in Dublin. After marrying Letitia, Henry bought a farm in county Kildare, a small village about 30 miles from Dublin. In 1872, Ireland was plagued by a potato famine. Since potatoes were a major crop in Ireland, the famine left farmers poor and starving. Henry was finally forced to sell his farm and pursue another career. He re-enrolled at Trinity College to study to be a doctor. After he graduated with a medical degree in 1884, the family moved to London, England. At first, Henry opened a practice in Croydon, but he then moved his office to Sydenham, an affluent suburb in southeast London. Although Henry made a modest living as a doctor, the Shackleton name was well-respected. His ancestors had a coat of arms, a family emblem often depicted on a shield, and a motto: *By perseverance we conquer.*

When Ernest was a child, his mother became sick with a mysterious illness that left her practically an invalid. Letitia spent much of her waking hours in bed, leaving Henry to raise the children. During his childhood, Ernest was schooled at home by a governess. When he was 11 years old, he began attending nearby Fir Lodge Preparatory School. In 1887, at age 13, Ernest studied at Dulwich College. Although an avid reader of both books and poetry, he did not do well in school. He later blamed his academic struggles on Dulwich's inadequate teachers. In an article for the school magazine, he said that Dulwich had taught him little in the areas of geography and literature. "Teachers should be careful not to spoil [the] taste of poetry for all time by making it a task and an imposition," he warned, as quoted in his book *South*.

Still, he did not let his classroom troubles ruin his love for reading. His favorite pastime was paging through *Boy's Own Paper*, a weekly magazine full of tales about adventures on the high seas. These stories carried Ernest's imagination to faraway places, across miles of jutting blue waves. He dreamed of joining the Royal Navy. However, his father could not afford to send him to Dartmouth College, the naval academy. Besides, Ernest was already too old to be admitted there. Henry had a cousin who was the superintendent of the Mersey Mission to Seamen. He managed to get Ernest into the Merchant Navy, working for Northwestern Shipping Company. For Ernest, who just wanted to be on the sea, it was a dream come true. On the other hand, his father hoped the harsh job as a sailor would make Ernest

NELSON'S SIGNAL AT TRAFALGAR.

Leading a fleet of British ships into battle against both the French and the Spanish, Lord Nelson ordered a special signal to read "England Expects That Every Man Will Do His Duty." This patriotic tale of heroism and bravery struck a chord with the nation and was featured in *Boy's Own Paper*, a weekly magazine that published stories of naval battles and explorations. Although Shackleton was not much of a student, he was an avid reader and enjoyed the publication.

dislike the sea. He wanted his son to follow in his footsteps and become a doctor. Ernest later wrote in *South*, "My father thought to cure me of my [desire] for the sea by letting me go in the most primitive manner possible as a 'boy' on board a sailing ship at a shilling a month."

In April 1890, at age 16, he set sail on his first sea voyage from Liverpool to Valparaiso, Chile, in the square-rigged *Hoghton Tower*, a three-masted clipper ship. A teenager on the high seas, Ernest made his first acquaintance with the sea and its wild temper. "I can tell you Nic," he wrote in a letter to a school chum, "that it is pretty hard work, and dirty work too.

It is a queer life and a risky one . . . you carry your life in your hand whenever you go aloft, in bad weather; how would you like to be 150 feet up in the air; hanging on with one hand to a rope while with the other you try to get the sail in . . . and there is the ship rocking, pitching, and rolling about like a live creature. . . ." It was a hard and difficult trip, one that would stay etched in Ernest's memory forever.

The *Hoghton Tower* rounded Cape Horn in the middle of the southern winter. Gale-force winds snapped some spars (round wooden or metal poles that support the sails) and injured several crew men, but young Ernest had a safe trip. The captain liked Ernest's grit and fire for the sea, although he also described him as "the most pig-headed and obstinate boy I have ever come across." Ernest stood apart from the other sailors in his habits and manners. On board, he read the Bible and quoted poetry, and he refused to drink alcohol, which was unusual for any sailor at that time. This first sea journey sparked a vision of greater adventure in Ernest. As the ship pushed around the Horn, the crew fought one continuous blizzard the whole way. "Yet many a time," Ernest later recalled, "even in the midst of this discomfort, my thoughts would go out to the southward." On ancient maps, Antarctica was labeled the "unknown southern land." Already, as a teenager, Ernest began setting the stage for his future as an explorer.

A Tale of the Sea

Having made it through his first voyage, Shackleton now had to decide whether or not he would pursue a life at sea. It was the first great decision of his life. "I think if I had hated the sea, I should have still stuck to it," he said years later. "But I didn't hate it, although I found it a hard life." And so, he became a ship's apprentice in order to one day qualify as an officer.

By age 20, Shackleton had already sailed around Cape Horn five times and earned the rank of second mate. At 22 years old, he was promoted to first mate. Two years later, he was a certified master, qualified to command British ships on any sea. For five years, he sailed on steamers between the Far East and America, to China, Japan, South Africa, and exotic Mediterranean ports. Captivated by the wind and the waves, he wrote a poem titled "A Tale of the Sea."

Although he had conquered any fear of the sea, he wanted more. He told a shipmate, "I think I can do something better. I would like to make a name for myself." Perhaps part of his ambition came from a desire to impress one of his sister's friends, Emily Dorman—the daughter of a prosperous Sydenham salesman. Like Ernest, Emily adored poetry, and before long, they fell in love. In 1899, Ernest took a position on the Union-Castle Line, one of the elite of the Merchant Navy and the next best thing to the Royal Navy itself. His relationship with Emily probably prompted the switch. The Union-Castle Line came home every two months, instead of making the long and undetermined voyages Shackleton had been sailing on. His new job took him down the Solent (a strait of the English Channel) from Southampton, round the bulge of Africa, across the Bight of Benin, into the docks of Cape Town and back again—6,000 miles each way.

In December, after being promoted to third officer, he was transferred to *Tintagel Castle*, which had been hauling troops to the Cape since the start of the Boer War in October. Dressed in a regal navy uniform with gold braids dangling from the shoulders, Shackleton served as an officer on the transport ships that carried soldiers to the war in South Africa. With his habit of quoting poetry, he was already an unusual type of officer. His interests seemed to span much wider than most of his companions.

In March 1900, Shackleton met army lieutenant Cedric Longstaff. Cedric's father, Llewellyn, was the chief benefactor of a proposed National Antarctic Expedition, the first British imperial venture to the far south in 60 years. Longstaff arranged a meeting between Llewellyn and Shackleton. Impressed by the young man's ambition, Llewellyn promised to use his influence to secure a place on the expedition for Shackleton. Because the expedition was primarily for members of the Royal Navy, without Longstaff's help, Shackleton might never get such a grand opportunity. As it turned out, Shackleton had more than one person pulling for him. The Royal Geographical Society (an organization that supports research for geographers and finances expeditions) was also a major sponsor of the expedition. Sir Clements Markham, the society president, took notice of Shackleton's intelligent and unusual personality. He was so struck by Shackleton that he may have chosen the young officer to lead the expedition. But Shackleton was in the Merchant Navy, not the Royal Navy, so the position went to another seaman—Robert Falcon Scott.

At this time, exploration of the Antarctic was a popular topic around the world. For Shackleton, the idea had been spinning in his head since his first sea voyage as a teenager. Shackleton later said that the unexplored parts of the world "held a strong fascination for me from my earliest recollections." But strangely enough, the event which actually inspired him to become an explorer was a dream he had when he was 22 years old. He later described it:

> We were beating out to New York from Gibraltar, and I dreamt I was standing on the bridge in mid-Atlantic and looking northward. It was a simple dream. I seemed to vow to myself that some day I would go to the region of ice and snow and go on and on till I came to one of the poles of the earth, the end of the axis upon which this great round ball turns.

Early in March 1901, Shackleton returned to Southampton on the *Carisbrook Castle*, part of the National Antarctic

Shackleton, who dreamt of exploring the unknown and reaching either the North or South Poles, had his first opportunity to reach Antarctica aboard the *Discovery*. Led by Captain Robert Falcon Scott (*above*), an officer of the British navy, the *Discovery* was a research expedition partially funded by the government.

Expedition. Shackleton would depart with Scott on the historic Discovery Expedition to Antarctica later that summer. Ernest was eager to embark on a journey that would become a tale of the sea like no other before, more fantastic than the adventures he had read about as a child.

On the Waves
of *Discovery*

THE DISCOVERY EXPEDITION'S LEADER AND CAPTAIN, ROBERT Falcon Scott, was in charge of selecting a 47-man crew for the mission. He appointed 36-year-old Albert Armitage, an officer in the Merchant Navy, to serve as second-in-command and navigator of the expedition. In 1894, Armitage had accompanied Frederick George Jackson and six others on the Jackson-Harmsworth Expedition to Franz Josef Land, a series of islands near the North Pole. They spent three years in a hut within the 80-degree-north circle, shooting polar bears and conducting scientific research. The highlight of the expedition was the resurfacing of Fridtjof Nansen, an explorer who had been missing in the Arctic for three years. One day when Armitage was out searching the area, he spotted two men approaching on skis. As they moved closer, Armitage recognized one of them as Nansen. Nansen explained that he and his companion had left his saucer-like ship, the *Fram*, and its crew to make a dash for the North Pole. Unfortunately, they soon discovered such a trek would be impossible. They set up a winter hut and lived on bear meat at latitude of 86 degrees 13 minutes north (86°13'N), the farthest north that anyone had ever gone. The two men had been dragging sledges and two kayaks, having eaten all their sled dogs by this point, across 700 miles of ice, hoping to reach Spitzbergen, a port where whaling vessels occasionally docked. Because of Armitage's valuable knowledge of polar exploration, he was a wise choice as navigator.

Scott invited along another member of the Jackson-Harmsworth Expedition—Dr. Reginal Koettlitz, a 6-foot-tall German with a drooping mustache. However, like many doctors at the time, Koettlitz believed that scurvy, the plague of all polar expeditions, was caused by a type of food poisoning. In his mind, the remedy for the deadly disease was absolutely pure food. In reality, scurvy is caused by a vitamin C deficiency. The only way to prevent or cure scurvy is to eat foods rich in vitamin C, such as vegetables and fruits—which were obviously hard to come by in the frozen Arctic. The assistant surgeon, Edward Adrian Wilson, would also be joining the expedition.

The three naval officers appointed were Charles Royds as first lieutenant in charge of dealing with the men and the internal economy of the ship, Michael Barne as second naval lieutenant, and Reginald Skelton as chief engineer. There were also three scientific positions on the expedition. Thomas Vere Hodgson, the director of the marine biological laboratories in Plymouth, accepted the post of naturalist. Hartley Ferrar served as the expedition geologist, and Louis Bernacchi became the expedition's physicist.

Shackleton was the only member of the expedition that Scott had not hand picked. Still, Shackleton was a respected officer, so Scott had confidence in his abilities.

The ship itself was built by Dundee Ship Building Company and it was one of the last big wooden sailing ships to be made in Britain. It was the sixth ship to be named *Discovery* but the first to be specifically designed and built for scientific work. The ship had to be constructed of wood, because steel would simply buckle under the pressure of the ice. Needing to be exceptionally strong, *Discovery* was built from a variety of timbers. The frame was shaped from 11-inch-thick English oak, and 11-inch-thick Riga fir was used for the lining. A second lining, four inches thick, was made of Honduras mahogany, pitch pine, or oak, and it was all sheathed with two layers of planking—26 inches of solid wood in all. Some of the bolts that ran through the hull were eight and a half feet long. The vessel stood an impressive 172 feet long and 34 feet wide. Although a sailing ship, it was also equipped with coal-fired, steam auxiliary engines. Not enough coal could be carried along, so sails were needed to conserve the coal supply. There was room enough in the ship to store fuel, oil, 350 tons of coal, fresh water, dog food, medical supplies, scientific instruments, axes, saws, other tools, sections for a wooden hut, and even a piano and a library.

The *Discovery* weighed anchor on July 31, 1901, and sailed down the Thames River. As the ship passed the shore on its way to the unknown, Royal Geographical Society president Sir Clements Markham noted, "No finer set of men ever left these shores, nor were men ever led by a finer captain." Emily's father wrote to Ernest, "I sincerely & heartily wish you a safe voyage & a happy return some 2 or 3 years hence having accomplished the arduous task before you & that you will be able to tell us what the Antarctic really is."

Reaching Antarctica

On January 2, 1902, *Discovery* crossed the Antarctic Circle. The next day on deck, the crew peered out at what seemed like a never-ending sheet of ice—what polar explorers call the ice pack. For the first time, Ernest experienced the striking and

Because his family could not afford to send him to a prestigious naval academy in Britain, Ernest Shackleton instead joined the Merchant Navy. With recommendations from Llewellyn Longstaff and Sir Clements Markham, Shackleton was able to secure a position on the *Discovery* (*above*), for a research expedition to Antarctica.

unforgettable sights and sounds of Antarctica. As Nansen once described,

> In its details it has forms changing interminably, and colors playing in all shades of blue and green . . . the drifting ice, a mighty white surface, curving into the distance as far as the eye can see . . . I will never forget the first time I entered this world . . . something white suddenly appeared . . . the first ice floe. More came; they appeared far ahead, with a squelching sound they glided past and disappeared once more astern. I noticed a strange glow in the [sky], strongest on the horizon, but it continued far towards the zenith . . . at the same time there was . . . a distant rumble as of surf beating on a shore. It was the pack ice ahead; the light was the reflection that its white surface always throws against the humid air.

This sight is called the "ice blink" of the polar navigators—a warning of the distant pack. "The sound came from the waves breaking against the floes," Nansen continued, "which cannoned against each other grinding and groaning; on still nights, it can be heard far out to sea."

Such was the frosty white world into which *Discovery* sailed. This voyage was not the only expedition on its way southward, however. On the other side of the continent, Otto Nordenskjöld was heading for Graham Land aboard his ship, *Antarctic*. One day, Shackleton would take Nordenskjöld's route. Nordenskjöld, a Swede, was the opposite of Captain Scott. Scott was a servant of officials, appointed by others, while Nordenskjöld had organized his own expedition, financed from private funds. Therefore, Nordenskjöld, not Scott, was the true polar explorer of the era. Likewise, Nordenskjöld was better prepared than Scott for such an expedition. He had already been to Greenland and led an expedition to Patagonia. Aware of his own weaknesses, Nordenskjöld also took along a Norwegian whaling captain and crew on the *Antarctic*, for their experience with the ice. About the same time as *Discovery* entered the ice pack, the *Antarctic* was grappling with the pack in the Weddell Sea.

Meanwhile, the *Discovery* pushed through the pack ice guarding the Ross Sea. One day, when *Discovery* became stalled in the pack, Scott decided to start training his inexperienced polar travelers. Shackleton, together with everyone else, except Scott, was ordered onto a nearby floe to start learning how to travel on the ice. With an audience of seals and penguins, the men tried their best to move about on their skis. Undoubtedly, these creatures watched in bewilderment as the crewmen fumbled, stumbled, and tumbled. "I think my share of falls was greater than the others," Shackleton bleakly wrote in his diary. Scott's crew made it through the pack in four days, one of the fastest of the seven passages on record at that time.

On January 8, the *Discovery* nosed out of the pack ice into the open water of the Ross Sea. The clouds also finally scattered after a long spell of gray and dreary skies. In the early morning, Shackleton saw the midnight sun, a phenomenon that occurs in latitudes north and nearby to the south of the Arctic Circle and south and nearby to the north of the Antarctic Circle. In fair weather, the sun stays visible for a continuous 24 hours, mostly north of the Arctic Circle and south of the Antarctic Circle. The number of days per year with potential midnight sun increases the farther poleward one pushes. That day for the very first time, Shackleton laid eyes on Antarctica, the mountains of the Admiralty Range of South Victoria Land rising in the distance. About this first glimpse of the ice-covered land ahead, he wrote that "so few having seen it before, makes us almost feel like explorers."

The next day at Cape Adare, Shackleton accompanied the landing party that went away in one of *Discovery*'s whalers to leave a message for a relief ship at Borchgrevink's base there.

This scrap of frozen tundra was Shackleton's first Antarctic landing. When the party returned to the ship, *Discovery* headed down the coast of South Victoria Land through treacherous polar waters. On January 20, Shackleton led a party ashore to examine some rocks at a place later named Granite Harbour. There, Reginald Koettlitz, the senior surgeon and botanist, identified some moss covering the base of a boulder. At 76°30'S, it was the most southerly plant ever found. Shackleton later recorded the event in his diary.

> Seeing some green stuff at the foot of a boulder I called [Koettlitz] to have a look at it. He went down on his knees then jumped up, crying, 'Moss! Moss! I have found moss!' I said, 'Go on! I found it!' He took it quite seriously, and said, 'Never mind, it's moss; I am so glad.' The poor fellow was so overjoyed that there were almost tears in his eyes. This was his Golconda*—this little green space in the icy South.

On January 22, *Discovery* reached Cape Crozier. Suddenly, the Great Ice Barrier burst into sight, a vast ice cliff stretching east from Cape Crozier as far as the eye could see. The barrier, nearly 400 miles long (600 kilometers) and about 1,000 feet thick (300 meters), had been discovered by Captain James Clark Ross in 1941. Originally called the Ross Ice Shelf, it is the point where the glaciers that flow from the Antarctic land mass begin to float on the sea, creating a cliff of ice.

Sir Clements Markham had ordered Captain Scott to follow the same route as Ross. On January 29, the *Discovery* at last passed Scott's farthest trek. Everyone on board was keyed up to be entering uncharted waters and undiscovered coast. In his

---

* In Shackleton's time, Golconda was an expression that meant something very valuable. Golconda was the old name of Hyderabad, in India, famous for its diamonds.

Shackleton's dream of becoming an explorer of uncharted territories became reality when he served as a crew member aboard the *Discovery*. As the expedition sailed toward and into Antarctica, floating ice complicated the journey and the men were forced to disembark and camp on the ice to wait out the end of winter (*above*).

diary, Shackleton called it "a very definite discovery." He wrote, "It is a unique sort of feeling to look on lands that have never been seen by human eye before." The complications of winter in Antarctica soon darkened the mood, though. On the evening of January 31, Shackleton took over the first watch, which went from 8:00 P.M. to midnight. He quickly realized that *Discovery* was faced with a serious situation. The ship was surrounded by icebergs on all sides.

Under these circumstances Captain Scott probably should have stayed on the bridge, he was below deck. He had simply left orders to continue east. The previous officer of the watch had blindly obeyed the orders and soon lost his bearings. He had sailed through a narrow entrance and no longer knew where he was. In the constantly shifting ice, the entrance could close up in an instant, leaving no escape.   In fact, it already had.

When Shackleton reported for his turn at watch, he re-alilzed that the ship was trapped. With or without orders, his only concern was to escape. He steered the *Discovery* round the

LIFE IN A SLEDGING CAMP

Life in a sledging camp was bitingly brutal. Polar explorers experienced some of the harshest conditions known to man. When setting up a sledging camp, the men set up small tents, just large enough for three men to lie down. They packed snow around the outside edges to hold it down in case of a sudden blizzard, which was common in Antarctica. Then, the men unloaded the sledges and set up a cooker inside each tent. When grabbing the metal cookers, they had to be careful. Any exposed skin would freeze right to it.

Changing from day gear into night gear was a laborious task. Each crewman carefully removed his finneskoes, or fur boots, making sure to leave them in the shape of his feet. In just a few minutes, the boots would freeze as hard as bricks. If the finneskoes were misshapen, the explorer would have to find a way to thaw them in the morning before he could pull them on. Next, he had to unlace his leggings, which had to be done with bare hands. At 40 degrees below zero Fahrenheit, he had to take breaks to stuff his hands into his pants and warm them up to keep from getting frostbite, which at these cold temperatures would set in in a matter of minutes. With boots and leggings off, each man layered three pairs of socks, which he kept next to his body all day in order to keep them warm. Then, he pulled on a long pair of fur boots that reached above the knee, followed by fur trousers and a fur night shirt. He tucked his day socks inside his pant leggings to keep them warm for morning.

(Continues)

(Continued)

Once dressed for bed, the men ate a supper of a hoosh—a dish made of pemmican (a mixture of fat and protein), cheese, oatmeal, pea flour, and bacon. After supper, the men climbed into their sleeping bags—three to a bag. At 40 below, it was much easier to keep warm with more than one man in a sleeping bag. On the other hand, one man could not move without disturbing the others. Condensation from breath was another problem in the tent. After a few days, the inside of the tent became covered with a layer of ice. Every time the wind shook it, a shower of ice rained down on the men inside. Also, their wet breath froze in their beards and around the necks of their fur coats, creating a collar of solid ice.

Another challenge, rarely talked about, was trying to go to the bathroom. An actual bathroom was out of the question. It took too long to dig a deep hole, and, besides, the hole would quickly fill back up with blowing snow. So each man would take his turn loosening his clothes and stepping out onto the icy tundra. Facing the blasting wind, he waited for a lull and pulled down his pants. No matter how quick he was, his pants would still fill up with snow. For the next few hours, he would battle the agony of a cold, wet bottom. Some of the men suffered from dysentery—a digestive illness that causes diarrhea. One can easily imagine the misery these men had to endure when blizzards raged for days on end.

bay in search of a passage out. When Scott emerged on deck at midnight, Shackleton had still not succeeded. At once, Scott flew into a panic. Shackleton tried to explain what was happening, but Scott was so unnerved he could not get a grasp on their predicament. Eventually, Shackleton went below, leaving the next watchman to deal with Scott. Shackleton came to the conclusion that the *Discovery* would winter in the ice, then the following summer, the group would head south over the frozen land on their polar exploration. In the meantime, a suitable wintering spot had to be chosen. After some time, *Discovery* nosed through the ice and hurried back along its tracks to the west. By February 8, Scott had returned to the waters under Mount Erebus, where the crew had caught first sight of the Great Ice Barrier. He announced that they would winter here, up the wide waterway of McMurdo Sound.

The western shore of McMurdo Sound runs along the edge of South Victoria Land. Ross Island was on the eastern side, under Mount Erebus. As *Discovery* moved up the 30-mile waterway, it seemed as though the expedition were sailing through some eerie dreamland. Tongues of ice jutted out of the western shore, mottled by volcanic grit. To Scott, the ice forms looked like tombstones in a cemetery. Finally, *Discovery* dropped ice anchors at 77° 50'S.

As the crew set up camp, Scott made plans for a march toward the South Pole. Scott chose scientist Edward Wilson and Shackleton to accompany him. The inclusion of Shackleton indicated a high level of trust by Scott.

Southward Sledge

FINALLY, ON NOVEMBER 2, 1902, THE JOURNEY SOUTH BEGAN. Scott, Wilson, and Shackleton set out together, with a large supporting party under Michael Barne following behind. As soon as they started, they were slowed by sticky snow and the deep sastrugi—a long wavelike ridge, or drift, of snow caused by the wind on the polar plains. Their skis sunk in about eight inches with each step. A two-day blizzard confined them to their tents. On the third day, Shackleton developed a hacking cough.

To make matters worse, the dogs did not want to cooperate. No one in the party was experienced in dog driving. Other polar explorers praised their huskies, impressed by their determination, stamina, and tenacity. With all the trouble Scott's party had, someone might wonder if they were using the same animals. However, Scott's dogs had been horribly mishandled. For one thing, they were cruelly underfed. Even though there had been seal for the taking, the dogs had been deprived all winter of fresh meat. Instead, they had been forced to eat a starvation diet of dog biscuits. Still, even if the dogs had been in peak physical condition, the party would not have been any better off. Shackleton and the others did not know that a dog's natural gait, when pulling, is a trot—a pace that matches the pace of skiing. However, neither Shackleton, nor anyone else on *Discovery*, could really ski. They plodded along instead of sliding. So the dogs were forced to walk, which did not suit them at all. Before long, the dogs lost all respect for their masters, and a dog will only serve those whom he respects. On this journey, Shackleton acquired a mistrust of dogs and dog driving that would have profound consequences on his future explorations.

At the seventy-ninth parallel (the circle of latitude 79 degrees south of the equator), half of Barne's supporting party turned back. The remaining group pushed on until November 15, when the rest of Barne's party gave up as well. Scott, Shackleton, and Wilson pressed farther. On November 25, 1902, they crossed the eightieth parallel, beyond which all maps were blank. "It has always been our ambition to get inside that white space and now we are there so the space can no longer be a blank," Scott wrote.

Things continued to worsen on the sledge, partly because of Scott's incompetence. When they had first started the trip, the party had enjoyed cooking and eating without limit. By the beginning of December, after a month of sledging, Scott suddenly realized that, without rationing, food and fuel would not last. From that point on, cooked meals were cut from three per day to two. Food was drastically rationed. Their full daily ration gave them about 4,200 calories. For the grueling trek, hard work, and cold temperatures, even that amount was too little. They probably should have consumed another 1,000 calories a day.

Hungry and tattered, the men obsessed about food. Shackleton wrote in his diary, "We always dream of something to eat when asleep. My general dream is that fine three-cornered tarts are flying past me upstairs, but I never seem able to stop them.

Billy dreams that he is cutting sandwiches for somebody else always. The Captain—lucky man—thinks he is eating stuff, but the joy only lasts in the dreams for he is just as hungry when he wakes up."

Perhaps the dogs suffered most of all, though. Their diet was abruptly switched from biscuits to stockfish alone. Aside from other essential nutrients, they were now deprived of fat. To make matters worse, the fish was spoiled too much for even the tough, scavenging gut of a dog. One by one, the poor animals sickened.

After seven frustrating weeks, they reached the eighty-first parallel on December 9. Now, Scott made a desperate decision to dump much of his load, including all the dog food. Traveling light, they would make a dash for the south, killing the remaining dogs along the way for food.

Meanwhile, Dr. Wilson noticed that Shackleton's gums were swollen—the first sign of scurvy. Plus, he still suffered from a nagging cough, although he tried to hide it from the others. He did not want the party to have to turn back because of him. Wilson, who also had swollen gums, became anxious about getting back. Still a mysterious disease, scurvy had one certainty—if left untreated, it was a killer. Wilson believed this symptom would be the one argument that could force Scott to turn around before it was too late.

Much to Wilson's distress, however, Scott insisted on going farther. They had not yet made it to the eighty-second parallel—the magic line Scott was determined to cross, no matter what. On Christmas Day, the three men argued about whether or not to push on. Wilson managed to get Scott to promise to turn around on December 28. Still, this meant another week farther away from home base, even after knowing that scurvy had appeared. On December 28, they made it to 82° 10'S. At last, they had crossed Scott's magic circle. But Scott went back on his word. He still wanted to go farther.

After mooring the *Discovery*, the crew packed up their supplies and dogs and set off on a journey to reach the highest possible latitude in Antarctica. Lacking survival experience, the men began to suffer from disease and struggled to use their sled dogs to their advantage. Pictured left to right, Ernest Shackleton, Captain Robert Scott, and Dr. Edward Wilson celebrate Christmas on the Antarctic continent.

They were at the mouth of a large inlet running west into the mountains on their right, about 270 miles from base. During the next couple of days, the winds picked up, making it nearly impossible to gain much ground. By December 30, they had made it to 82°15'S. This point was as far as the party would go. That afternoon, Wilson and Scott left a weakening Shackleton alone to guard the camp while they walked out to look at the inlet. They made it to 82°17'S. That was to be their Farthest South. Shackleton's however, remained at 82°15'S.

Although they had not gotten as far south as they had hoped, Shackleton knew they had accomplished a great feat—gaining about 300 miles of new coastline. "It is a wonderful place and deserves the trouble . . . it takes to get here," he wrote.

And, they had beaten the record for the south by more than 200 miles.

Race Against Death

The misery the explorers had suffered on their way south was nothing compared to what awaited them on the return journey north. It would be a race against death to get back to the base alive. Along the way south, they had laid depots at various points where they had buried food and supplies. It was over 100 miles to the first depot. They needed to get there by January 17 or they would run short on food. Although the depot was located by landmarks in the mountains to the west, the exact location would be hard to find. The place was marked by a single flag, which could have been covered over with snow by now. There was a chance they would miss it altogether. The midnight sun was dipping lower in the sky. Soon daylight would run out completely.

On the first day, the homeward march seemed to be going well. They trampled along under clear skies and a following wind. After four miles, Scott wanted to stop and set up camp, then wander off to the west for some geological samples from the bare cliffs on the coast. Reluctantly, the other two men agreed. However, crevasses stopped them from making it to the cliffs. The excursion cost them half of a day that could have been spent traveling. The dogs, as Shackleton said, were "done for." The few battered dogs that had survived this far were only a hindrance for the others. The men yoked themselves like oxen to the sledges, while the dogs walked along beside them. The snow was so heavy that it took all their strength to trudge a mile in an hour. They had given up on trying to battle with the skis and decided to plod all the way back to the base on foot.

Hungry, tired, and weak, the three men lumbered north. Sometimes they would suddenly break through the ice crust and drop knee-deep into the loose powdery snow beneath. On the morning of January 10, 1903, they were still 33 miles from the first depot, a good four days' march. Their food, they hoped, would last, but there was not enough to allow for any setbacks. At this critical time, a blizzard weighed in. They knew that it was march or die, so they groped their way through the drift, barely able to see their hands in front of their faces.

Shackleton's health continued to worsen. Although he was short of breath, he refused to admit his deterioration, even in his diary. In fact, on January 13, Shackleton was out in front of the group. "I steered," he said, "by the sastrugi." (The wind-blown ridges follow the prevailing wind, which in this case was south to west. Shackleton used this knowledge to keep him moving in the right direction.) That afternoon, they spotted the depot flag. Their cheers sounded more like moans, but at least they had food to eat. That night they ate a hearty meal. The meal did little to boost Shackleton's energy, though. He started coughing up blood, and they were still 160 miles from the ship, with full loads to pull all the way.

The men tried to cut their loads, tossing everything they could possibly sacrifice. As they trudged out from the depot, Shackleton could barely keep up. After two miles, they were forced to set up camp. Shackleton was too sick to go any farther. All night long, he coughed and gasped for breath. From that point on, Shackleton was forbidden to do any sledge pulling. That left the entire load of more than 500 pounds for the other two to haul. Luckily, any symptoms of scurvy in Wilson and Scott seemed to be subsiding. However, other aches and pains, like swollen joints, were steadily increasing. Nevertheless, they were better off than Shackleton. At least they could stay steady on their feet.

In his diary, Shackleton tried to be optimistic about his grave condition. "Hope to be in full swing . . . tomorrow," he wrote on January 17. On the other hand, Wilson tells a much darker tale. "Shackleton had a very bad night [and] a bad day and was not allowed to pull," wrote Wilson. "The moment he attempts a job he gets breathless and coughs." At the same time, all three men knew they could not carry him on the sledge.

Reaching the next depot, like the first one, was a race for life. A hundred miles lay in between. In order to get there before food ran out, they had to march seven miles a day. Because the men were walking, not skiing, they sometimes broke through the snow into buried crevasses. Luckily, their harnesses saved them, but the falls were dangerous for men with scurvy. Brittle blood vessels are symptomatic of the disease. Each fall could cause a hemorrhage. On January 16, Shackleton fell into one of these hidden crevasses. The fall left him badly shaken. For several hours, he felt sick and groggy.

On January 25, the steam-pluming tip of Erebus appeared over the horizon. That meant the ship was only about a week's march away. Three days later, they were nearing the final depot. Like the other one, it was marked only with a single flag. Just as every inch of visibility was vital, a blizzard set in. Fortunately, during a lull in the gale, they spotted the depot flag. Although still 60 miles from the ship, they had all the food they needed. At last, their fear of starvation had ended. Shackleton, however, did not feel much relief. All day, while the blizzard roared, he lay in the tent, struggling for breath. That night, Shackleton was restless and unable to sleep. He overheard Wilson tell Scott he did not expect Shackleton to last through the night. Hearing those words made Shackleton even more determined to make it back to camp.

The next morning, Shackleton was still alive, yet so weak he could barely speak. Throughout the day, Shackleton took breaks from marching and rode on the sledge. Again, he made it through the following night, wheezing and gasping for air. He was coughing up blood again. On February 3, six miles (seven kilometers) from the ship, they caught sight of

Reginald Skelton and Louis Bernacchi hurrying out to greet them. The two men hardly recognized their captain and shipmates. "Long beards, hair, dirt, swollen lips & peeled complexions, & bloodshot eyes [which] made them almost unrecognizable," Bernacchi wrote in his diary. "They appeared to be very worn & tired & Shackleton seemed very ill indeed."

Beracchi and Skelton insisted on hauling the sledge the last few miles to the ship. To their astonishment, the load which seemed such a strain for Scott and Wilson was actually no trouble at all. Back at *Discovery*, the crew threw a welcome home party for Scott, Wilson, and Shackleton, but Shackleton was too exhausted to join in the celebration. "I turned in at once when I got on board," he wrote, "not being up to the mark, after having had a bath—that is the first for ninety-four days. It is very nice to be back again; but it was a good time."

Of course, Shackleton's entry seems grossly understated for someone who had scarcely survived. But his desire to be a polar explorer was growing stronger with each passing day he endured on the ice-crusted coast of Antarctica. However, his days with the *Discovery* quickly came to an end. A relief ship had arrived at McMurdo Sound 10 days before Shackleton and the others returned to base camp. At this point, *Discovery* was still frozen in its winter haven. Four miles (six kilometers) of solid ice stretched between the ship and the nearest open water. It was February, and winter in the Southern Hemisphere was approaching. *Discovery*'s ice prison would never thaw before winter arrived. Clearly, the crew would have to stay another year. Scott decided that Shackleton was too sick to make it through another winter.

When the relief ship *Morning* set sail on March 2, 1903, Shackleton was on board due to his ill health—the greatest disgrace for an explorer. As the ship set off to sea, Shackleton stood on deck, watching the edge of the ice slowly slip farther away. He wrote, "Ah me it was sad parting . . . snow was falling, and a dreariness seemed over all things . . . the sun came out in a blaze of glory and bathed the bergs in lights that were more than splendor: the small waves twinkled in the sunlight; waves not seen by me for more than [a] year . . . Mount Discovery away down South from us was a splendid sight standing out in the clear blue of the Southern sky. It was so familiar my home fading away. I turned in a read for a bit but thoughts would go back to those I left on the floe."

When Shackleton returned to England, he tried to reenter the life he had known before the Discovery Expedition. Even

SIR ROBERT FALCON SCOTT

British naval officer and polar explorer Robert Falcon Scott was born on June 6, 1868, at Devonport, Devon. In 1880, at the age of 13, he passed his entrance exams to begin his naval career as a cadet on the naval training ship H.M.S. *Britannia*. Two years later, he became a midshipman. In 1887, he was promoted to first lieutenant. About this time, he caught the attention of Sir Clements Markham, president of the Royal Geographical Society—the principal promoter of British exploration. In 1899, Markham chose Scott to head the National Antarctic Expedition on a dash to the South Pole.

In August 1901, the *Discovery* set sail for Antarctica. For two years, the ship anchored off Hut Point, Ross Island, in McMurdo Sound. On Dec. 30, 1902, Scott, Shackleton, and Edward Wilson reached latitude 82°16'33"S—the farthest south record up until that point. A year later, Scott reached latitude 77°59'S, longitude 146°33'E. The expedition drew to a close when the *Discovery*, with the relief ships the *Morning* and the *Terra Nova*, reached New Zealand in April 1904.

In 1909, Scott announced new plans to reach the South Pole. With support from Markham and the British government, the *Terra Nova* sailed in June 1910. While at sea, Scott learned that Roald Amundsen though he was thrilled to see his family and Emily, he longed to be winter bound with the rest of the expedition. Until Scott returned, however, Shackleton had to try to set aside his burning desire for polar exploration. In the fall of 1903, he was hired as a sub-editor for the *Royal Magazine*. Although he possessed cleverness with words and creative ideas, he had no real experience in journalism, except editing a newspaper for the Discovery Expedition—*The South Polar Times*. On January 11, 1904, Shackleton was elected to the post of secretary to the Royal Scottish Geographical Society. He now had a

and his Norwegian party were also attempting to reach the pole. A race for the pole had begun. From winter headquarters at Cape Evans (latitude 77°38'24"S), Scott began his sledge journey on Nov. 1, 1911.

He had placed much faith, too much as events were to prove, on motor sledges and Manchurian ponies. The motor sledges broke down and, one by one, the ponies died. Even before they left the last supporting party at latitude 86°32'S on Jan. 4, 1912, Scott's pole party was already in trouble. On January 18, Scott's party reached the South Pole only to find the Norwegian flag, a tent, and a note from Amundsen. The Norwegian party had reached the goal on December 14, 1911.

Heartbroken, starving, and weary, the party now turned back to base camp. Suffering from scurvy, frostbite, and exhaustion, his men faced a race against death. On March 29, 1912, Scott and the remaining three members of his party (one man had died earlier) reached latitude 79°40'S. Eleven miles from One Ton Depot, the men made camp for the last time. On March 29, Scott wrote his final journal entry, knowing he was about to die. Eight months later, a relief expedition found the tent, bodies, journals, and records.

Scott and his men had survived the heroic journey to the South Pole but sacrificed their lives in the process. The tragic death of Scott and his men shocked the world. However, the appalling news was not enough to deter Shackleton, who was already planning his next expedition.

With the *Discovery* surrounded by frozen ice, miles away from open water, Captain Scott and his crew decided to stay through the winter to wait for the spring thaw. Unfortunately, Shackleton's ill health prevented him from completing the expedition and he returned home aboard a relief ship. *Above*, Shackleton's last sighting of the *Discovery* crew as he sailed away.

full-time job and could think about marrying Emily. "I am so happy dearest thinking about all the times which are to be in the future," he wrote her. "We do want to settle down and have our own house at last after all these years of waiting." In London, on April 9, 1904, Shackleton and Emily Dorman were married at Christchurch, Westminster.

In early April, the *Discovery* at last returned to New Zealand after her second season in the ice. The record Farthest South, in which Shackleton had participated, still stood. But Shackleton was restless to go back to Antarctica. He had already formed grander visions of his next voyage. "I want to go on a further expedition soon," he said. "This time I want to command it myself."

Nimrod Expedition

In the late 1800s, the British Empire had made colossal territorial expansions. Oddly, the government spent little on exploring, conquering, and expanding the white spaces on the map. In some isolated cases, rich amateurs or industrialists backed expeditions. But gaining support for polar expeditions proved difficult for Shackleton. Few businessmen believed that wealth could be gained from the Antarctic. Any funding for polar exploration usually had to be based on motives more nationalistic than economic. Ever since he returned from the Discovery Expedition, Shackleton had been dreaming of returning to Antarctica. Even the birth of his daughter, Cecily, on December 23, 1906, did not steer him away from his ultimate dream. Three days later, he wrote, "I see nothing of the old *Discovery* people at all. We are all scattered, and the fickle public are tired of the polar work at present. What would I not give to be out there again doing the job, and this time really on the road to the Pole!"

About this time, there were rumors of the French and Belgians forming expeditions. Shackleton decided to sweep into action. He approached William Beardmore, a stern, no-nonsense industrialist. Beardmore had made his fortune by being careful and working hard. But he also had a generous nature. Moreover, Shackleton had managed to charm Beardmore's wife, Elspeth, who probably lobbied on his behalf. Beardmore eventually signed a guarantee for 7,000 British pounds—not a huge sum, but enough for Shackleton to get moving. Before he could make a public announcement of his intentions, however, he had to break the news to Emily.

Up until this point, Shackleton had kept his plans for launching an expedition somewhat secret. Unless he secured financial backing, he knew that his plan would remain a dream, and he did not want to needlessly worry Emily. Now, with a baby only weeks old, he had to tell her that he would be leaving for one or two years. "You can imagine that it was with mingled feelings that I sent the wire to you that the Expedition was settled," he wrote her. "It will only be one year and I shall come back with honor and with money and never never part from you again. . . . I am just longing to hold you and tell you that you will be a part of history." Emily—always Shackleton's greatest supporter—offered him encouragement on his race for the pole.

The night of February 11, 1907, was a special evening for the Royal Geographical Society and anyone interested in polar exploration. That evening, the headline speaker was Roald Amundsen, who had remarkably completed the Northwest Passage, a treacherous route that snaked between the Canada mainland and the Canadian Arctic islands. For 300 years explorers had been trying to navigate through the Canadian archipelago. Amundsen had finally done it in a tiny ship with only six companions. Later that night, an announcement revealed that not one but two Antarctic expeditions would be launched. One of them was Henryk Arçtowski's Belgian

Anxious to return to Antarctica, Shackleton lobbied and raised money to fund an expedition. On this ambitious journey, Shackleton planned to employ the use of sled dogs, Siberian ponies, and even a new Arrol-Johnston motorcar specially produced for the trip (*above*).

expedition that Shackleton had heard rumors about, and the other was Shackleton's.

The very next day, Shackleton had a public announcement printed in the newspaper. In the article, he indicated that his party would leave that same year and winter at the old hut on Ross Island. After dropping off most of the crew, the ship would return to New Zealand to avoid being frozen in and then pick up the wintering crew the following summer. In the meantime, Shackleton and his companions would try to reach both the Geographical South Pole and the South Magnetic Pole. The South Magnetic Pole is the wandering location where the south-seeking end of a dip needle—a bar magnet suspended freely on a horizontal axis—points vertically down toward Earth's center. Shackleton went on to explain that in addition to dogs, Siberian ponies would be taken along. In his opinion, the surface of land or ice was suited for this mode of sledge traveling. Also, he would introduce a new vehicle—a specially designed motorcar.

Shackleton planned to set sail in a matter of months, and he had to pull together an entire expedition—a ship, supplies, more financial support, and a crew. First, he turned to his old colleagues from *Discovery*. One by one, however, they turned him down, even his friend Edward Wilson. Before long, Shackleton discovered the reason: Scott was considering another expedition to the South Pole. Scott was enraged when he heard of Shackleton's plans, thinking Shackleton was being underhanded. He wanted to keep Shackleton out of the territory and forbid the use of the old base at McMurdo Sound.

> [I]t must be clear to you now that you have placed yourself directly in the way of my life's work—a thing for which I have sacrificed much and worked with steady purpose," he wrote Shackleton. "If you go to McMurdo Sound you go to winter quarters which are clearly mine. . . . I do not

like to remind you that it was I who took you to the South
or of the loyalty with which we all stuck to one another or
of incidents of our voyage or of my readiness to do you
justice on our return.

Scott's words sparked a heated exchange between the two
explorers. To claim the rights of an entire region was absurd,
and Shackleton knew it. Also, it burned Shackleton when
Scott claimed to be so close with the members of his party.
Scott's insistence on pushing south had nearly killed them
all. Furthermore, Scott had sent Shackleton home against his
will, causing great embarrassment for the explorer. To add
insult to injury, Scott's book painted a weak picture of Shackleton. He claimed that Shackleton had to be carried on the
sledge because he was too sick to walk, when Wilson's diary
clearly contradicted these claims. In part, Scott's accusations
fueled Shackleton's already intense desire to prove himself in
the Antarctic. He was prepared to endure anything—even to
risk death.

These two strong personalities collided in a fierce struggle of wills. Luckily, Wilson entered the picture as a mediator
and tried to smooth things out. Even though Scott's expedition would not take place for another two years, Wilson urged
Shackleton to give up the base at McMurdo Sound. Bending
to the influence of his friend, Shackleton sent a cable to Scott
on March 4, stating, "Will meet your wishes regarding the
base . . ." Instead, Shackleton said he would seek a base in
King Edward VII Land, to the east of the Great Ice Barrier. By
giving up the base, Shackleton thought that one major issue
had been resolved. He was terribly wrong.

Within days, he received another message from Wilson
advising him to hold off on any plans until he had heard from
Scott. Scott wanted to put limits on Shackleton's rights to ex-
plore. This time, Shackleton put up more of a fight. He fired
back in writing:

There is no doubt in my mind that his rights end at the base he asked for. . . . I will not consider that he has any right to King Edward the Seventh's Land, and only regard it as a direct attempt to keep me out of the Ross quarter if he should even propose such a thing. I have given away to him in the greatest thing of all, and my limit has been reached. . . . You know as well as I do that I have given up a certainty almost for a very uncertain base as regards to the ultimate success of the Pole. . . . I consider I have reached my limit, and I go no further.

In May, Shackleton and Scott met face to face to discuss their differences. In the end, Shackleton agreed, in writing, to avoid the McMurdo Sound base and land either at Barrier Inlet or King Edward VII Land—whichever was most suitable. If he landed at either of these spots, he would not march to the west of 170 degrees west and promised to not make any sledge journey going west of that meridian unless circumstances prevented him from taking a different route.

Scott was enormously pleased with Shackleton's agreement. In essence, he and Wilson had bullied Shackleton into accepting extraordinary conditions. In truth, they should have never even made such outrageous demands, ones that might impact the safety of Shackleton's entire expedition. Nevertheless, the agreement had been made. At least Shackleton could now devote his full attention to his preparations.

Outfitting a Sealer

Shackleton chose the name British Antarctic Expedition of 1907 for his polar trek. He opened an office at 9 Regent Street, at the edge of Waterloo Place in London's Clubland. After hiring a business manager—Alfred Reid, who had assisted previous polar ventures—Shackleton went to work sorting out the multitude of details for the expedition.

At the outset, he consulted Fridtjof Nansen, the explorer who had gone missing in the Arctic and an experienced sage of travel and survival in the polar regions. His unrivalled success in the far north made him a valuable source of information and advice. Nansen gave Shackleton expert advice on food, clothing, cooking equipment, and transportation. He also offered some tips on working with dogs and skis, as well as the benefits of using animal fur for clothing and sleeping bags. Shackleton should have followed Nansen's recommendations exactly. But on two crucial points, he veered away from Nansen's advice. Shackleton's poor decisions cost him dearly.

Shackleton disagreed with Nansen in the use of dogs and skis. No doubt, his hesitation to use them stemmed from his disastrous experience with them on the Discovery Expedition. Instead, he decided to use horses. While horses were used on other polar explorations, they suffered from numerous problems. The pressure from their hooves broke holes in the ice, hard-crusted snow, and most dangerously—ice bridges over glacier crevasses. They also consumed massive amounts of feed and suffered from digestive problems, and grooming them away from camp was nearly impossible. In reality, many of the horses died on the expeditions. Still, Shackleton felt convinced that horse travel was the way to go, even though Nansen and other successful explorers had proved dogs to be such an enormous, life-saving asset in the Arctic. Unfortunately, Shackleton chose to blame the dogs on Scott's expedition instead of their masters.

The next issue was Shackleton's reluctance to use skis, although he did pack a number of pairs. Again, he was having trouble seeing past *Discovery* setbacks. He decided that if the motorcar and horses failed, he would fall back on man-hauling. So, he ordered 15 Manchurian ponies, more than the number of pairs of skis he set aside for the journey.

In Norway, Shackleton found the perfect ship for his expedition. *Bjön* (Bear) was a three-year-old seal ship, built exclusively for polar work. It weighed 700 tons and included berths for 50 men, vast storage space, and powerful triple-expansion engines that could easily fight the ice near King Edward VII Land. He wanted to purchase the ship immediately, but it was priced at a costly 11,000 pounds. At once, he returned to London to try to raise the money.

Meanwhile, Beardmore had taken over the only Scottish motor-car manufacturer, the Arrol-Johnston company of Paisley. In an effort to revitalize the failing company, Beardmore ordered a specially designed automobile for Shackleton's expedition. The car's chassis was specially treated to withstand extremely cold temperatures. The air-cooled engine topped out at 16 miles per hour, and the exhaust system was utilized for warming purposes. It operated on two fuel tanks—one fed by gravity, the other by pressure. Arrol-Johnston also constructed three different sets of tires for surfaces of varying hardness.

Although undoubtedly intrigued by the vehicle, Shackleton would much rather have used the construction cost to invest in his ship. Shackleton would not be able to purchase his dream ship, *Bjön*. Shackleton was forced to find a ship that better fit into his tight budget. Instead, he settled for a grimy little sealer from Newfoundland at a price of 5,000 pounds—the *Nimrod*. Built in 1866 of oak, green heart, and ironbark by the firm A. Stephens & Son, the *Nimrod* weighed a modest 334 tons. The ship was grossly underpowered, and whether or not it would stand up to the pounding fury and incessant storms of the Southern Ocean was questionable. Nevertheless, at this point, Shackleton had little choice.

When *Nimrod* arrived in the Thames on June 15, 1907, Shackleton was horrified. His new ship looked even smaller than its measurements made it sound. To make matters worse, it was a dilapidated mess—its masts rotten and every inch reeking of seal oil and filth. At once, Shackleton turned *Nimrod* over to the R. and H. Green shipyard in Blackwall with repair orders to make it seaworthy for some of the roughest conditions in the world. Shipyard workers thoroughly caulked the hull and scraped and cleaned the holds. They tore down the masts and rigging and transformed the ship from a schooner to a barquentine, with square sails on the foremast and gaff-headed fore and aft sails on the main and mizzen. New quarters for the crew were built and ice damage repaired. By July, *Nimrod* could sail at eight and a half knots and could make six knots under steam engine, burning four tons of coal a day in smooth water.

With the old sealer outfitted for the southern sea, *Nimrod* still needed a crew. Initially, all Shackleton's attempts to entice former members of *Discovery* failed. He finally managed to convince Ernest Joyce and Frank Wild to join the expedition. Shackleton appointed thirty-one-year-old Rupert England as captain. Although not his first choice, England had some Antarctic experience as first mate of the *Morning*. At second mate was Eneas Mackintosh, and Jameson Adams was Shackleton's second in command. Twenty-three-year-old John King Davis and twenty-year-old Sir Philip Brocklehurst—the youngest crewman—also signed on. Shackleton also employed James Murray as ship biologist. One of the two surgeons was Dr. Alistair Forbes Mackay. The senior surgeon was Dr. Eric Marshall. Raymond Priestly served as the expedition geologist, and Leo Cotton signed on as another scientist. Bernard Day, who was employed at Arrol-Johnston's Motor Car Company, joined the crew as motor engineer. The pastry chef at the Naval and Military Club—William Roberts—became the ship cook. And George "Putty" Marston agreed to be the expedition artist.

On August 7, 1907, the *Nimrod* finally departed England, sailing across the jagged waters of the Bay of Biscay to sweltering São Vincente in the Portuguese sugar colony of the Cape

Verde Islands. After re-coaling there, the ship made passage to Cape Town, South Africa. Then, the *Nimrod* embarked on the long haul across the Indian Ocean to Lyttelton, New Zealand, arriving in October. In Lyttelton, Shackleton suddenly realized that the *Nimrod* would not have enough coal to get to the Ross Ice Shelf and back. The ship would have to be driven by sail a good deal of the time. In fact, without good winds, the expedition might never get to King Edward VII Land at all. Worse, it might never make it home. In New Zealand, Shackleton employed Arthur Harbord as the auxiliary second officer.

With a square-rigged extra master's certificate, Harbord held the highest qualification possible in sailing ships, as well as those driven by steam. Hopefully, with Harbord's expertise, the expedition stood a fighting chance.

Broken Promise

Ballast is the heavy material placed in the hold of a ship to maintain stability. A basic in the maritime world, it threatened to destroy the entire British Antarctic Expedition. Shackleton figured he would be able to harness the wind to get the *Nimrod* to the Great Ice Barrier, but it would be no help in getting the ship back to New Zealand. A great deal of coal might have to be used to force through the pack ice on the Ross Sea—going both south and back north again. The coal was serving a dual purpose for the ship—as fuel and ballast. If the entire supply of coal was consumed, nothing would prevent the ship from capsizing in the heaving seas.

Shackleton's inexperience as a commander probably explained the oversight, but it certainly came as a devastating blow. He would have to come up with a new, creative alternative to deal with the problem. If the *Nimrod* could be towed to the Antarctic Circle, he decided, the ship could preserve enough coal to return under steam power while still providing the necessary ballast. Luckily, Shackleton's charm in his public appearances had won over New Zealanders. When he asked the government for help, New Zealand offered to pay half the cost of towing *Nimrod* to the ice. The chairman of the Union Steam Ship Company, Sir James Mills, picked up the other half and provided the towing ship, a steel-built steamer named the *Koonya*. A four-inch thick, steel wire hawser would be shackled to *Nimrod*'s chain cables for the pull.

When they set sail on January 1, 1908, they hoped for good weather. Because the *Nimrod* did not have much storage space, it was overloaded. It had only three feet of ship sitting above the waterline. Within an hour of reaching open sea, the tiny ship was swamped by massive waves. The crew was sailing into the fiercest gale any of them had ever experienced. During the following 10 days, the petite *Nimrod* was ruthlessly doused and battered. "I have never seen such large seas in the whole of my seagoing career," Arthur Harbord wrote. Inside the ship, every piece of cargo was crammed and crowded—man, pony, dog, and supplies.

On January 9, the storm reached its climax, reeling mountainous green waves as far as anyone could see. Every minute, the *Nimrod* was swept with a wall of water, from bow to stern. Shackleton ordered the crew to stay off the deck as much as possible. All the while, the ship was in serious danger of capsizing, tilting 50 degrees in one direction, then suddenly jolting just as far to the other. But it would be the last great tempest of their voyage. By noon the next day, the sky was fair and clear. At last, the men could begin drying out.

Finally, on January 14, icebergs appeared up ahead. The following morning, the crew could see a jagged-line of ice along the horizon. The *Koonya* had towed the *Nimrod* 1,400 nautical miles to the Antarctic Circle. Now, with no protection from the ice, the steel ship had to turn and head for home. A series of boat journeys between the two vessels had been planned to

The *Nimrod* was used for Shackleton's 1907–1908 expedition into Antarctica. Setting off from New Zealand, Shackleton hoped to conserve coal and had the ship towed toward the Antarctic Circle. On the way, the crew was caught in a fierce polar gale that whipped up the seas, causing the *Nimrod* to toss and turn in the water (*depicted above*).

ferry fresh water, coal, and the carcasses of 20 sheep to the *Nimrod*. However, the tossing waves made this impossible. Instead, crewmen on the *Koonya* threw a line to the *Nimrod* and managed to string over 10 sheep. But the winds and waves picked up and carried the line away, so the second half of the meat could not be transferred. All plans to convoy the rest of the provisions were also dropped, and the *Koonya* steamed north and out of sight.

The *Nimrod* continued south, toward what Shackleton assumed was pack ice. When the ship reached the line of ice in the distance, however, the men learned that it was not the pack at all. In front of them rose a stretching band of icebergs, unlike any they had ever seen before. Hundreds of them towered 150 feet tall and two miles long, forming a maze that the *Nimrod* now had to navigate through. Tannatt William Edgeworth David, another scientist who had joined the expedition in New Zealand, described the scene:

> Imagine countless huge blocks ... of pure alabaster or whitest Carrara marble above, shading into exquisite tints of turquoise and sapphire at the water's edge, and changing to a pale emerald green below the water ... we seemed to have entered the great silent city of the Snow King ...

The *Nimrod* spent the day dodging and weaving through this massive ice-mountain barricade before it suddenly burst into open water. A stiff breeze cut across the deck as the ship pushed through a thick blanket of snowfall. Shackleton and his men had made it to the Ross Sea, and in record time, even after being forced to penetrate a labyrinth of icebergs. However, they ended up in the territory that Shackleton had promised Scott not to cross. Shackleton turned southeast toward the barrier, far from McMurdo Sound, trying to at least uphold most of his promise.

Shackleton had decided to winter at what he now called Barrier Inlet, which was part of the ice shelf. His plan was innovative but also fraught with danger. No one had ever before dared to camp on the ice shelf. Chunks of the shelf often break away to become the drifting icebergs *Nimrod* had just passed by on the way to the Barrier Inlet. There was tremendous risk that the camp might get carried off to sea, far away from the ship and provisions.

On January 23, the barrier came into view. Shackleton explained to the others his tentative plans. After setting up the base, he, Adams, Joyce, and Armitage would go due south to lay depots for the next spring's march to the South Pole. Meanwhile, Marshall, David, Priestley, Marston, Wild, and

Mackintosh would take two ponies and go east to King Edward VII Land. Shackleton's plans, however, were hinged on finding Barrier Inlet. As it was just a thin slice in the shelf, this was not an easy task.

What looked like a smooth wall of ice from a distance turned out to have dark spots of deep caverns. The thin black lines on the shelf could be either shallow inlets or deep bays. By the next morning, Shackleton had spotted nothing that resembled Barrier Inlet. The ship moved alongside an ice floe—a medium-sized, flat-topped piece of ice floating on the surface. As Shackleton stared at the floe, he began wondering if he was in the right spot. After fixing their position, he learned that not only were they east of where Barrier Inlet ought to be, but they were at 78°20'S. In other words, the *Nimrod* was south of where, six years earlier, the barrier had stood in the *Discovery*'s way. Apparently, chunks of the ice shelf had broken off, taking Barrier Inlet with them.

Shackleton shuddered to think about the disaster that could happen if his crew set up on the ice and it broke away. He realized he had two options: to make an attempt on King Edward VII Land or to break his promise to Scott and winter at McMurdo Sound. He decided to continue east along an open waterway toward King Edward VII Land. However, the *Nimrod* suddenly became threatened by a large pack of mounded ice moving closer from the north. The ship would have to get away before it got trapped in the ice. Quickly, Captain England spun the *Nimrod* around and fled back the way they had come, shooting through a gap between the pack and the barrier with only 50 yards of open water.

At this point, Shackleton was ready to give up on King Edward VII Land and turn to McMurdo Sound. Some of his crewmen, however, did not want to dishonor Scott by going back on their word. Shackleton agreed to try once more to reach King Edward VII Land. All night, Captain England steered the

Nimrod east, only to be stopped once again by the pack. On the morning of January 25, the *Nimrod* changed its course for McMurdo Sound. Shackleton would have to deal with the consequences of his broken promise later. For now, he wanted to keep his men and his mission safe.

Great
Southern
Journey

As the *Nimrod* neared McMurdo Sound, Shackleton realized that the ice pack was blocking the way to Scott's winter base. Instead, *Nimrod* headed up the coast of Ross Island toward Cape Barne and a small hook north of it called Cape Royds. The *Nimrod* anchored here, and the crew built their winter quarters. They named it Hut Point. In 1904, Scott and Wilson had camped at this very spot while waiting for relief ships, and this would be the winter base for the British Antarctic Expedition. During the winter, Shackleton trained his men for the realities of polar travel. Weekly, he sent out different parties to haul supplies and food to Hut Point. Each party came back with stories to tell of cold, misery, adventure, and more cold. By late September, they had stocked the *Discovery* hut with enough supplies for the 91 days Shackleton planned for the Southern Party to be out on their journey for the pole. They also established Depot A at 79°36'S, approximately 120 miles

The Nimrod Expedition, led by Shackleton, established a camp at Cape Royds by building a cabin to house the crew, their supplies, and their ponies and dogs for the exploration (*above*). In 2005, several organizations announced a plan to refurbish the hut, along with several others from different expeditions, to preserve the history of exploration in Antarctica.

from Cape Royds—the one depot stocked with feed for the ponies.

On October 5, 1908, the Northern Party—David, Mawson, and Mackay—left the winter quarters, assigned to a task every bit as dangerous as the one undertaken by the Southern Party. Under Shackleton's instructions, their key objective was to take magnetic observations at every suitable point

CAPE ROYDS: NO PLACE LIKE HOME

Shackleton had no experience living in a hut in the far south. The men of the *Discovery* had wintered aboard ship. With this in mind, the new winter quarters at Cape Royds showed incredible foresight and planning on Shackleton's part. The hut was built to face northwest, looking at Pony Lake. Across the lake, there was an impressive view of McMurdo Sound and the western mountains. Next to Pony Lake stretched a flat sheet of ice that became snow covered during the winter. The men used this area, which they called Green Park, to exercise the horses and play football and hockey. Rectangular in shape, the hut was 33 feet by 19 feet. The men had built it with sections of fir timber and lined it with match-boarding. For insulation, the outside walls and roof were covered with heavy roofing felt, a one-inch layer of tongue-and-groove boards, and another layer of felt. As extra insulation, the four-inch space between the match-boarding and the inner felt was filled with granulated cork. For added protection against the strong southerly winds, the men stacked a wall of provision cases six feet high around the back of the hut. They also stacked provisions on both sides of the building.

Inside, the hut was divided between a common area and cubicles that offered a bit of privacy for the men. In order to save space and weight, Shackleton had brought practically no furniture. When they arrived at Cape Royds, the carpenter built some crude furniture pieces out of empty provision crates. A four-foot-wide stove burned anthracite coal constantly, both for cooking meals and keeping the hut somewhat warm. Although the stove could not heat the hut like a furnace in a house, it could keep the indoor temperature about 60 degrees above the outside temperature.

The men had some fun setting up their living spaces. They gave their cubicles names, such as No. 1 Park Lane, The Gables, and Rogues' Retreat. There was also a photographic darkroom and a print room. On the Discovery Expedition,

(Continues)

(Continued)

Shackleton had edited *The South Polar Times*. On this expedition, Shackleton decided his men would publish an entire book. The final copy was named *Aurora Australis* and featured 10 articles.

Throughout the seemingly endless winter, the 15 men at Cape Royds experienced plenty of agonies. Their diaries recorded how the cold, wind, and darkness interfered with every aspect of daily life, from taking scientific measurements to exercising the ponies to preparing meals. The hut was no place like home, but it certainly beat tenting in a sledge camp.

with a view of determining the dip and the position of the magnetic pole. If time permitted, they would also try to reach the magnetic pole. In addition, they were to conduct a general geological survey of the coast of Victoria Land and, on their way back, make a stop at Dry Valley to do some prospecting for minerals of monetary value. This job was especially important to Shackleton, because he hoped to discover some sort of polar treasure.

After they left Cape Royds, uncertain ice conditions forced them to start south toward Glacier Tongue before turning west and crossing to (what would be known as) Butter Point. This spot would be named by Scott's party for a ton of butter they had left there in a later expedition. Their plan was to head north along the coast of Victoria Land, hoping to find a passage up to the high Polar Plateau. Six years before, Albert Armitage had been the first to reach this point while Scott, Shackleton, and Wilson were on their southern adventure.

A blizzard slowed their travel, but the Northern Party finally reached Butter Point on October 13. The group realized that at their present speed, they had no hopes of making it to the magnetic pole, about 500 miles from Cape Royds, and return in time for the relief ship. Therefore, they left a depot of 70 pounds, 40 percent of which was biscuits, and a note warning they would not be back before January 12, 1909. Then they set off north across New Harbour—the wide, ice-covered entrance to the Ferrar Glacier and Dry Valley (known today as Taylor Valley). On October 17, they reached the northern edge of Cape Bernacchi, a low, rocky promontory. Here, they pitched a red and white flag, claiming Victoria Land for the British Empire.

Meanwhile, Shackleton was preparing for his journey south. The Southern Party consisted of Shackleton, Wild, Adams, and Marshall. A five-member support party made up of Joyce, Marston, Armitage, Brocklehurst, and Priestly would also travel part of the way to the South Pole. The men had tremendous faith in their leader, but they had no idea what his journey would require. "If we'd known what a high altitude they'd have to get to, I think we'd have had much more doubt as to whether they'd reach the Pole or not," Brocklehurst later wrote. "But Shackleton was so enthusiastic and so confident in his own ability that he didn't leave much for us to think other than success."

On the morning of October 29, 1908, Shackleton and his companions bid farewell to Murray and Roberts—the only men left at the base. They then turned south to begin what Wild called "The Great Southern Journey." The time had finally come, and Shackleton was bursting with enthusiasm as the horses lugged the sledges away from base. "At last we are out on the long trail after 4 years thought and work," Shackelton wrote in his diary. "I pray that we may be successful for my Heart has been so much in this."

Across the Barrier

The snow-covered barrier was soft and spongy. At times, the ponies sunk into the snow all the way to their bellies. Within a week, they had reached an area of the barrier scattered with deep crevasses. A driving snow made the chasms even more difficult to spot. Marshall and his pony, Grisi, almost disappeared down one crevasse. Worried about the safety of his men, Shackleton decided they must stop and wait for better weather.

Conditions did not quickly improve, however. The following day, a blizzard confined them to their tents. Because of the delay, Shackleton reduced their lunch rations to two biscuits in order to conserve food. "We must retrench at every setback, if we are going to have enough food to carry us through," he noted. They had started with 91 days of food, but with careful management, Shackleton believed they could make it stretch 110 days. Shackleton had calculated the South Pole to be 859 miles from Cape Royds. His party would have to travel almost 19 miles a day to reach it and return on the allotted food. Because of delays, they had only averaged about seven miles a day so far. By cutting down their daily food allowance, they would need to cover only 15 miles a day.

Finally, on November 7, Shackleton decided they must push on—even though the weather was still not ideal for traveling. The four men of the Southern Party said goodbye to the support party and continued on their march. The blowing snow made visibility nearly zero. Through the white wall, not even the shape of a cloud could be seen to help guide them. The group was still too far west, but a march east would invite certain disaster. With visibility so poor, they could not see a crevasse until they were on top of it. Within just an hour, each member of the party had stepped into a hole that could have meant the end of both him and his pony. At last, the group was forced to camp again. They remained still for almost 48 hours, tented between two deep crevasses.

The four men had to split into two tents. To prevent them from forming cliques, Shackleton rotated tentmates every week, as well as cooking duties. Sadly, neither Shackleton nor the others showed any understanding of horses. The ponies had constantly broken through snow crust that dogs would have lightly run across. Similarly, the men's weight would have been better distributed on skis. At the end of the day, the ponies were forced to camp outside, exposed to the bitter winds. While the Antarctic conditions would not have bothered the dogs, horses were not designed for this kind of weather. They had hides that helped release heat rather than retain it. The poor ponies suffered miserably.

On November 21, they passed 81°S and stopped for the night. There, they shot one of the ponies—Chinaman—whose fetlocks had been seriously frostbitten. They cut up the meat, leaving 60 pounds at Depot B and taking with them another 80. Before heading out the next day, they marked the depot with a single black flag on a spear of bamboo. From time to time along the way, they constructed snow cairns to help mark their way back home. On November 26, the explorers had passed the farthest south yet reached by any man. Shackleton had finally overcome the embarrassment of being sent home on the *Morning*. And he had done it in much less time than it had taken with Scott—29 days compared to 59 days. The prize of the pole seemed to be within their grasp.

From that day forward, the haul was entirely new. These sights had never before been seen by any human eyes, and their footsteps were the first human footsteps to touch this land. Huge new mountains towered in the clear sky, sheer granite cliffs rising thousands of feet over the snowy plain. It was a mystical sight—so unlike any other place known in the world.

Two days later, though, the party was delivered a heavy dose of reality. Another pony had to be shot. The horse meat offered more provisions, but the men were now down to two ponies. The increased loads on the remaining sledges meant they had to help the horses pull—more calories burned and painful hunger. Another worry was that the mountains, which had been off to their right, were curving east to cut straight in front of their path. Shackleton had hoped to find the South Pole on the barrier. He had not planned to climb any mountains. Equally distressing was the fact that the barrier itself was changing. It formed what seemed like deep sea swells with crests about half a mile apart. In between the crests, the snow was so deep and soft that the ponies could hardly move. One of the final two ponies became so exhausted from hauling that he had to be shot. The last pony spent the whole night howling in loneliness from the loss of his companion.

As they continued their march, they seemed to stumble at last on a shred of good luck. Directly south, there appeared to be a large glacier leading south between the mountains—the Golden Gateway to the south. In the distance, there was a low, snow-covered pass between the red mountain and a bare rock point three miles southwest of it. Beyond the pass, the glacier opened up through the mountains in an almost due south direction. When they set out in that direction, they soon found themselves in a sea of crevasses. The farther they trudged, the more crevasses they encountered until they reached an enormous chasm about 70 feet deep and 60 feet wide. Luckily, several hundred yards to the west of it, the chasm closed and they were able to continue. After six hours of dodging deadly crevasses, they reached the mountain and clambered up a rock face for a look south.

"There burst upon our vision an open road to the South," described Shackleton, "for there stretched a great glacier running almost South and North between the great mountain ranges." The passage extended as far as the eye could see, flanked on either side by rugged, ice-crusted mountains. The men speculated that this glacier, which they named "The Great Glacier" (today called Beardmore Glacier), must be the largest

Trekking across the frozen continent, Shackleton and his crew stumbled upon the Great Glacier, later to be renamed Beardmore Glacier (*above*) for a patron who helped pay for the expedition. Shackleton's discovery of Beardmore Glacier and the area around it would lead to future developments in paleontology, geology, and various other fields.

in the world—at least 30 miles wide and more than 100 miles long. However, from their lookout point, they could also see the mountains running far to the southeast. They realized that if they continued on the barrier, their way would be blocked by impassible heights. Still, they had found one of the few paths through the Transantarctic Mountains.

Navigating across the glacier was tricky business. Huge crevasses and frightening edges forever loomed ahead. On December 6, Wild suddenly stepped out into open space, and his heart pounded in a terrifying rush. He let out a muffled cry. Ten yards ahead, Shackleton and the others turned their heads to see what had happened. In an instant, Wild and his horse Socks vanished into the glacier.

Falls into the crevasses may have been horrifying, but they happened so often that the men got used to them. "The first few falls are decidedly upsetting to the nerves & heart," Wild had written in his diary. "To find oneself suddenly standing on nothing, then to be brought up with a painful jerk & looking down into a pitch black nothing is distinctly disturbing, & there is the additional fear that the rope may break. After a few dozen falls (I have had hundreds) the nervous shock lessens until the majority of men look upon the experience as lightly as an ordinary stumble."

This particular fall, however, was no ordinary stumble. When Shackleton and the others reached the crevasse, they could see the pony sledge hanging in the chasm, with Wild dangling off to the side. There was no sign of Socks. He had disappeared into the black pit. Miraculously, Wild survived, saved by the lead rope he had twisted around his wrist. The last horse was gone, but, thankfully, he did not take Wild and the sledge full of provisions down with him.

Now, the men would be forced to haul the sledge themselves. In the following days, they experienced the full wrath of the Great Glacier. The glacier was a slippery incline that seemed to never plateau. And the wide, cracked pressure ridges and ice falls that split in every direction forced them to climb and then haul the sledges up and across by rope—hand over hand. Even with the extra horse meat, they had to cut back on food if they would have any hope of reaching the South Pole.

On December 15, the party's hope soared. Out in front of them stretched a long, vast plain. At last, they could pick up their speed. "We hope to make a depot tomorrow of food and oil and all the gear we can spare," Wild recorded. "By the look of things we should be on the plateau the day after tomorrow, and then 20 days of good going ought to put us at the pole. We are now very hopeful of doing the job and of getting back in time to catch the ship." However, the plateau was not as close as it seemed. Several more days came and went, and they still were not clear of crevasses, slogging uphill through soft snow.

Food allowances continued to be cut. With their physical labor, they should have been consuming at least 6,000 calories a day but were only eating 2,500. Then, after weeks of brilliant weather, the conditions turned nasty. A hard, cutting wind picked up from the south, blowing directly into their faces day after day. By this time, the men were all getting on one another's nerves. They were hungry, tired, cold, and weather-beaten. However, they did their best to keep their feelings confined to their diaries. Wild wrote of Marshall, "I sincerely wish he would fall down a crevasse about a thousand feet deep. He certainly does not pull the weight of the extra tent and his kit, and that leaves the weight of his food for us to pull."

The four men sat in one tent on Christmas Day, assessing their situation. They were just short of the 86°S latitude, about 280 miles from the South Pole. As things stood, they did not have enough food to reach their target and make it all the way back to base, even with the depots. Their solution was to once again cut their daily food intake. "We are going to make each week's food last ten days and have one biscuit in the morning, three at midday, and two at night," wrote Shackleton in *The Heart of the Antarctic*, his expedition diary. "It is the only thing to do." He also noted another worry. "Marshall took our temperatures tonight. We are all two degrees subnormal, but as fit as can be."

The next morning, they ditched everything they did not absolutely need. With the limited food supply, they would need to make 14 miles a day. At least the lightened load helped ease the burden of their uphill march. After a couple more days, they finally reached the plateau, leaving the crevasses behind them. Yet they continued to make a slow ascent. By December 27, they had passed 10,000 feet above sea level. The increasingly thinner air caused other health concerns—light-headedness and prolonged headaches. At this point, the party confronted some serious obstacles: a fierce headwind, more than 40 degrees of frost, and a horrible sledging surface. Then, on December 29, Marshall found all their temperatures to be between three and four degrees below normal. The men realized they would not make it to the South Pole. Instead, they decided to push as far south as they could before turning back.

However, a blizzard held back the rush. The men were freezing and starving, their tents were wearing out, their clothing needed regular repair, and their sleeping bags were too damp to protect them against the temperatures that plunged to 15°F below zero. Their lack of food had not given them the strength they needed to make the climb up the glacier. "We are so tired after each hour's pulling we throw ourselves on our backs for a three-minute spell," Shackleton wrote. Still, Shackleton continued to be optimistic, but the others grew doubtful.

On January 1, 1909, the group was forced to stop just a mile short of the record for the southernmost latitude ever reached on the planet. In 1906, Robert E. Peary had claimed the farthest north latitude at 87°6'. But Shackleton suffered such a debilitating headache from the altitude that he could no longer march. The following morning, however, they beat Peary's record, as they plodded ahead for ten and a half geographical miles. But this distance was far short of the average they needed to make it to the pole. That night in his diary, Shackleton sounded the first hint of defeat. He admitted that even if a man's spirit prevailed, his physical limitations might be vanquished. He wrote:

> God knows we are doing all we can, but the outlook is serious if this surface continues and the plateau gets higher [they were already at 11,034 feet above sea level], for we are not traveling fast enough to make our food spin out and get back to our depot in time. I cannot think of failure yet. I must look at the matter sensibly and consider the lives of those who are with me. I feel that if we go on too far it will be impossible to get back over this surface, and then all the results will be lost to the world. We can now definitely locate the South Pole on the highest plateau in the world, and our geological work and meteorology will be of the greatest use to science; but all this is not the Pole. Man can only do his best, and we have arrayed against us the strongest forces of nature.

For a brief moment the next morning, it looked as if there was still a chance as they stumbled on some good hard surface. But the surface quickly turned soft again. On the night of January 3, the four men held a meeting in the wind-whipped frozen little tent pitched at 87°28'S, 152 geographical miles from the South Pole. They all agreed that it was beyond their grasp. However, they decided to make one last throw of the dice to get a bit farther. They would depot most of their provisions to lighten their loads and push south as fast as they could. The following morning, Shackleton and his three companions set off on the riskiest gamble ever—a dash to get within 100 geographic miles of the southernmost spot on Earth.

It was a brutal feat. At an altitude of 11,200 feet, and with the temperature lurking at negative 20°F, the men struggled against an icy wind. At noon, Marshall took their temperatures. None of them even registered on his clinical thermometer, which went down to 94°F. At the time, the medical community believed that anyone with a temperature lower than 94°F was already dead. They may have looked and felt like the walking dead, but they were certainly still alive. They made it twelve and a half miles, but they had hoped to do better. They could go no faster hauling 70 pounds than they had lugging 200. It was more proof as to how much they had physically weakened.

The next day was more of the same. Their feet sank eight inches with each step. The winds picked up and the temperature dropped. Nevertheless, they managed to make it another 13 miles. But the worst was yet to come. On January 6, the temperature plunged to 57 degrees of frost and the wind reached blizzard strength. Frostbitten and exhausted, they were forced to make camp at 4:30 that afternoon. They had reached 88°7'S. Shackleton decided they only had one more march left in them.

Finally, on January 9, the winds began to ease. By four in the morning, the group was ready to make the final dash. They stuffed some biscuits and chocolate in their pockets, grabbed Queen Alexandra's flag, a camera, and a brass cylinder holding some special stamps issued by the New Zealand government to help raise money for the expedition. They marched as fast as their legs would carry them. The cold and the blizzard had made the surface solid and firm for quick marching. They pounded south, at times almost running. Five hours later, they halted at 88°23'S, 162°E. They had passed the magic hundred-mile mark—in fact only 97 geographic miles from the South Pole. Although it was only an estimation (they had left the teodolite in camp to save weight), it was a figure that would go down in history as fact. Shackleton planted the Union Jack and took

After surviving some close calls, Shackleton's four-man expedition group set a new record when they came within less than 100 miles of the South Pole. Because they were dangerously low on rations, the crew established their presence with a flag and headed home after taking a few photos (*above*).

possession of the region for Great Britain, naming it the King Edward VII Plateau. After taking two photographs and burying the tin of stamps, the party turned north for the first time in months. "Homeward bound at last," Shackleton wrote that night. "Whatever regrets may be, we have done our best." They had beaten the Farthest South record by 366 miles.

Desperate March

The four men were more than 700 miles from Cape Royds. They had a limited amount of time to reach Hut Point before the *Nimrod* would leave. In addition, their food supply was running dangerously low. "Rush we must now," Wild recorded. "We have only 14 days short food to take us to our depot at the top of the glacier . . . a great part of it over pressure and crevasses."

By January 16, the Transantarctic Mountains gradually came into view. From this point on, the four men made only brief journal entries. They no longer had the energy to write lengthy accounts. In order to help them move faster, they used the sledge floor cloth as a sail. When the wind was whipping from the south, they could make more than 20 miles in one day. If they had been still traveling toward the South Pole, this same wind would have kept them from making good headway. Although the sail helped move them along, the gusts caused the sledge to buck like an unbroken horse. The four men practically had to run to keep up with it, spending valuable energy.

They were pleased with their distances, yet exhausted. They raced across crevasses, two men roped ahead of the sledge and two unroped steering at its sides. Somehow Shackleton managed to keep up the pace even though his heels were cracked from frostbite. "I don't know how [Shackleton] stands it," wrote Wild admiringly. "Both his heels are split in four or five places, his legs are bruised and chafed, and today he has had a violent headache through falls, and yet he gets along as well as anyone." The worse he felt, the harder he pulled. He used brute determination to get him to the next depot.

By January 24, they were still 40 miles from the depot, with food for only two days. Luckily, the next day they blasted down the glacier, making a blue-ribbon pull of 26 miles. At breakfast on January 26, they finished the final crumbs of their food bag, figuring they would be at the depot that afternoon. They calculated wrong.

Immediately upon leaving the camp, they were faced with a series of pressure ridges, between which rolled waves of soft snow that made pulling incredibly tough. Before noon, the terrain transformed into a maze of crevasses thickly covered with new snow. The men had to take their time and watch their footing carefully. Their lunch break offered only a cup of tea with the last spoonful of sugar.

By midafternoon, they were stumbling from hunger and exhaustion, trudging through a white plain of snow 12 to 18 inches deep. They were marching less than a mile an hour. At 5:30 that night, Marshall dug out a handful of "Forced March" tablets, which contained a cocaine preparation to help keep them on their feet. Still, they could hardly drag their feet above the snow. Each hour, Marshall fed them another dose of tablets. At ten that night, they added a cup of cocoa to their tablet and managed to struggle on. By two in the morning, Marshall's wonder drugs were gone, and the men were falling asleep on their feet. When Wild finally collapsed, they were forced to camp just three miles from the depot.

After a long nap, they started on their way again. This time, Adams collapsed. A short while later, he was able to move again. By one in the afternoon, though, the entire party was wiped out and had to stop. They had been without any solid food for 30 hours. "I cannot describe adequately the mental and physical strain," Shackleton wrote. He referred to the forced march as "the hardest and most tiring days we have ever spent in our lives."

While Shackleton watched over Adams and Wild, Marshall set off toward the depot to bring back food. Twenty-five minutes later, he was there, after narrowly escaping three falls into crevasses by hurling himself forward and grasping for the edge just as he felt his feet go through. Marshall collected four pounds of pony meat, cheese, pemmican, biscuits, and tobacco. For energy, he ate two lumps of sugar to help him make it back. He decided if he had to choose between Forced March tablets or sugar, he would definitely pick sugar. Within the hour of leaving the party, Marshall returned, and the men were feasting at last on a real meal.

The following morning, they made it to the depot, where they gobbled down another hefty meal. They reached the barrier by three that afternoon, making 14 miles, only 50 to 60 miles from Grisi Depot. With the Great Glacier behind them, they had entered the final stage. The next day, a thick snow began to fall and the temperature rose to 32 degrees. The snow melted on the men and the sledge immediately after it had landed, saturating everything. Suddenly, a cold wind picked up, dropping the temperature by 20 degrees, freezing solid everything that had gotten wet. The men had no other choice but to stop and warm up. When conditions failed to improve, they were forced to wait out the blizzard—using up more valuable time.

Finally on January 30, the blizzard lifted. But by this time, Wild had developed dysentery, a digestive disorder that causes severe diarrhea. He could barely stagger along. They could wait no longer, though, so they headed out. Remarkably, by the end of the day, they had progressed 13 miles and had not met a single crevasse. Meanwhile, Wild continued to grow weaker. The medicine Marshall gave him made him so drowsy that he fell asleep on the move. His stomach was so sensitive, he could not eat horse meat or pemmican, and there were not enough biscuits for him to have extra. Shackleton secretly gave Wild his biscuit ration. His gesture meant so much to Wild that he underlined every word he wrote about it:

> [Shackleton] forced upon me his one breakfast biscuit, and would have given me another tonight had I allowed

him. I do not suppose that anyone else in the world can thoroughly realize how much generosity and sympathy was shown by this; I DO, and BY GOD I shall never forget.

When the party reached Grisi Depot, they were once again almost out of food. That night, they feasted on pemmican and meat hoosh. The next day, however, another disaster let loose. All four men were hit with "Grisi's Revenge." Perhaps the horse meat was spoiled because Grisi the horse was in such a dilapidated state when he had been killed, or maybe they had not cooked it long enough. Either way, they all felt horribly ill—having to stop as many as 13 times in 24 hours due to sour stomachs. That day, they only advanced five miles.

On any other day, the morning of February 4 would have been a perfect day for sledging. It was calm and sunny, yet not so warm that it affected the snow. Nevertheless, all four men lay moaning in camp, their stomachs painfully cramping. Finally, the next day, they were able to move again.

On February 22, they came across tracks of a party of four men, with dogs. They assumed it must be Ernest Joyce, who was supposed to have left provisions for them at the final depot. All they had to do was follow the tracks to the depot. That night, they camped only 12 miles from where they figured the depot must be. The next morning, in anticipation of reaching it that day, they wolfed down all their remaining food. They headed in the direction of the depot, but it did not appear. Their stomachs dropped, as they realized they may have finished up their food stores foolishly. Then, suddenly, Wild caught sight of the depot flag—far off in the distance, barely above the horizon.

The depot was not as near as they wished, though. They did not reach it until four that afternoon. Finally, their fears of starvation had ended. That evening, they savored delectable treats they had not tasted in months—plums, eggs, cakes, gingerbread, and crystallized fruit. For dessert, each man took back to his sleeping bag a selection of sausages, chocolates, and jams.

One fear gone, a new nightmare began. It was now the night of February 23, 1909. Shackleton had left instructions with Murray to leave with the ship if they did not return by March 1. While three men with supplies would still stay behind at Cape Royds and wait for them, Shackleton and his companions did not really want to spend another winter isolated in the Antarctic. If the men could not make it back within six days, they would be marooned.

On the trek to the South Pole, it had taken them more than a week to make it from Hut Point to where they now camped. Going back, they planned to take a longer route—going farther east to avoid the crevasses near White Island. There was no time to waste. The first day, they made 15 miles. When they arose the next morning, Marshall was too sick with dysentery to travel. They were tent-bound the whole day. The next day, they pounded ahead 24 miles, but the intense march had taken its toll on Marshall. Still, they pushed on. On February 27, they made good progress until four in the afternoon, when Marshall suddenly collapsed.

They were still 33 miles from their destination with only 36 hours left before the *Nimrod* would sail without them. After pitching a tent, Shackleton left Marshall in the care of Adams, and he and Wild stormed north, taking with them nothing but a compass, sleeping bags, and food. After a brief dinner break, they plowed ahead until two in the morning. By late morning, they were still plodding along, having long since finished the small amount of food Adams had packed for them.

The final stage of their march would finish the same as it had been spent—struggling for each footstep, enduring painful hunger, and battling the endless snow and wind. Suddenly, at four in the afternoon, nature hurled its last mean blow—the sky clouded over, a fierce wind rose, and a blizzard spun drifts of snow in every direction. Shackleton and Wild could barely see each other. While the stormed whirled around them, they had to walk through an area of pressure ridges and deep crevasses. As they neared Hut Point, their stomachs sank. The *Nimrod* was not there. No one was in the hut. Nailed to the window, a letter explained where everyone had gone. The ship would shelter under Glacier Tongue until February 26. Nothing more was written. Shackleton and Wild stared silently at the piece of paper in front of them. Despite all their efforts, the *Nimrod* had left them behind.

Rescued

Shackleton and Wild refused to give up hope. If they burned an old hut, perhaps someone on the *Nimrod* would see the fire and come rescue them. However, they could not get anything to burn. Then they ran up the hill to Vince's Cross—a place set up in honor of George Vince, the sailor who had died on the *Discovery* expedition. They tried to tie the Union Jack to it, but their fingers were too cold to make a knot. Overcome by hunger and cold, the men returned to the hut and made dinner with the supplies there. Finally, at nine the next morning, Shackleton and Wild managed to set the hut afire and put up the flag.

Meanwhile, the *Nimrod* had sailed south to land the wintering party and find the bodies of the Southern Party. Suddenly, though, someone spotted two men standing on Hut Point waving a flag. Shackleton and Wild were saved, but there were still two men out on the barrier, and Shackleton planned to rescue them—himself. As he and Wild boarded the ship, he immediately took charge of the situation. After a dinner of bacon and fried bread, he put together a party to rescue his men. Shackleton had been on the move for more than two days straight, without proper sleep for 55 hours. Still, he had no intention of letting someone else do his job. Leaving Wild behind, he took Mawson, Mackay, and Thomas McGillion and headed back out across the barrier. They marched for seven and a half hours before stopping for a dinner that Shackleton prepared while the others rested. After a short nap, they were up again at two in the morning, pushing full speed until they reached Adams and Marshall early that afternoon.

THE WANDERING POLE

While Shackleton was marching toward the Geographic South Pole, the Northern Party of Edgeworth David, Douglas Mawson, and Alistair Mackay was inching its way toward the magnetic pole. Day after day, the ice around them slowly decayed. On one side of them the sound gradually broke up. They lived in constant fear that the ice might break off and sweep them out to sea. So, with agonizing sluggishness, they edged along the snow-covered ice made sticky by the sea salt. More than once, the men discussed giving up the plans of reaching the magnetic pole to instead focus on gathering scientific data.

At the end of October, the men stashed a letter in an empty dried-milk tin and tied it to a flag staff. The letter, addressed to Shackleton, said that the party hoped to reach the "low sloping shore" by December 15. This spot was marked on the admiralty chart as north of the Drygalski Ice Barrier, now the Drygalski Ice Tongue. There, they would construct a depot and march inland to the magnetic pole. Around January 25, 1909, they would return to the depot at the low sloping shore. As the

In the early morning of March 4, 1909, the rest of the party was aboard the *Nimrod*. The ship turned north and sailed away from Cape Royds. Later, Shackleton wrote,

> We all turned out to give three cheers and to take a last look at the place where we had spent so many happy days. The hut was not exactly a palatial residence . . . but, on the other hand it had been our home for a year that would always live in our memories. . . . We watched the little hut fade away in the distance with feelings

three men would soon discover, though, no area of low sloping shore actually existed.

When they reached the Drygalski Ice Barrier at the end of November, they were shocked to find out it was entirely different than they had expected. The surface was formed of jagged ice, very heavily crevassed. They realized this glacier was absolutely impossible to cross by sledge. Still, on December 1, they started over the glacier, which David described as "high sastrugi, hummocky ice ridges, steep undulations of bare blue ice with frequent chasms impassable for a sledge." After three hours of hard labor, they had only gained half a mile. They pushed on, and by December 9, Mackay finally spied the sea north of the ice tongue. They were almost across the ice barrier and near their goal.

The going continued to be rough—a treacherous labyrinth of pressure ridges and crevasses. Finally, at noon on January 15, 1909, Mawson took some magnetic measurements. They were near the magnetic pole. Because the magnetic pole wanders, Mawson suggested waiting where they were for 24 hours, so the pole might come to them. But they decided to push on the 13 miles to where they predicted it would be. On the morning of January 16, they hoisted the Union Jack at 72°15'S, 155°16'E, at an elevation of 7,260 feet. They snapped a picture and, wasting no time, turned back for home base.

almost of sadness, and there were few men aboard who did not cherish a hope that some day they would once more live strenuous days under the shadow of mighty Erebus.

Marooned in Antarctica

ON JUNE 14, 1909, SHACKLETON RETURNED TO ENGLAND A
national hero, just as famous as if he had actually reached the
South Pole. The Royal Geographical Society presented him
with a gold medal for his amazing accomplishment. The British Parliament settled Shackleton's expedition debts, and he
was knighted by King Edward VII. He wrote a book about his
adventure, *The Heart of the Antarctic*, and went on a lecture
tour that took him all over the British Isles, the United States,
Canada, and much of Europe. All the while, his thoughts wandered back to the Antarctic.

Meanwhile, an American expedition under Robert E.
Peary had reached the North Pole in 1909. Then Scott, on his
second expedition in late 1911 and early 1912, was raced to the
South Pole by Norwegian explorer Roald Amundsen. Amundsen beat Scott by a little more than a month. Scott also reached
his goal. But on the return march, he and his three companions, weak with scurvy, died trying to make it back to their

When Shackleton returned home after completing the Nimrod expedition, he was greeted as a national hero and knighted for his extraordinary accomplishment. Shackleton's explorer's mind, however, was soon wandering back toward Antarctica as his rivals set new records. American explorer Robert Peary (*left*) reached the true North Pole the same year Shackleton (*right*) and the *Nimrod* crew came within 100 miles of the South Pole.

base. News of Scott's tragic death saddened all of England. The nation's loss held an extra sting, because the British came in second to Norway in the process.

Shackleton had been making plans to win back the nation's honor. Once, he had promised Emily he would never go on another expedition again. But she knew there was no way to keep him home. "How could you keep an eagle tied in a back-yard?" she asked. Shackleton had been within 97 miles of the South Pole. For him to repeat the same trek would be nonsense. Besides, he had already set his sights on something bigger. "I feel that another expedition—unless it crosses the continent—is not much," he wrote in a letter to Emily.

Shackleton felt that the first crossing by land of the Antarctic continent, apart from its historic value, would be a journey of great scientific importance. The distance would be roughly 1,800 miles. The main party would sail to the Weddell Sea, land a shore party in the Vahsel Bay region on the western coast of Antarctica to prepare for a march via the South Pole to the Ross Sea. From the Ross Sea base in McMurdo Sound on the east coast, another party would push southward to lay depots and await the arrival of the transcontinental party at the top of the Beardmore Glacier. Meanwhile scientific parties would collect specimens and operate from a base on the Weddell Sea.

Two ships would be needed for the expedition. Shackleton bought the *Aurora*, a stoutly built sealing ship that had already been on two Antarctic expeditions. This ship would carry the Ross Sea party, under the command of Lieutenant Eneas Mackintosh, who had served on the *Nimrod*. Shackleton would command the actual transcontinental party operating from the Weddell Sea. His ship had been named the *Polaris*, but Shackleton rechristened it the *Endurance*, after his family motto: "By endurance we conquer."

THE *ENDURANCE*

By any standards, the *Endurance* was a beautiful ship. It had been built in Sandefjord, Norway, by the Framnaes shipyard, famous for polar shipbuilding. A barkentine, it consisted of three masts—the forward one square-rigged, while the following two carried fore-and-aft sails, like a schooner. Powered by a coal-fired, 350 horsepower steam engine, it was capable of driving at speeds of up to 10.2 knots. Overall, it measured 144 feet long, with a 25-foot beam, which was not overly huge but big enough. From the outside, its sleek black hull looked much like any other vessel of similar size. However, it was not.

The *Endurance* had been designed for maximum strength. Its keel members were four pieces of solid oak, one above the other, adding up to a total thickness of seven feet one inch. Its sides were constructed of oak and Norwegian mountain fir, varying in thickness from about 18 inches to more than two and one half feet. Outside this planking, to keep it from being chafed by the ice, the ship-builders attached a sheathing from bow to stern made out of greenheart—a wood so heavy it weighs more than solid iron and so tough it cannot be worked on with ordinary tools. Compared to a regular ship, the frames were not only double-thick—ranging from nine to eleven inches, but there were also twice as many. The *Endurance*'s bow, which would meet the ice head on, also received special attention. Each of the timbers had been fashioned from a single oak tree especially selected for its natural growth, which followed the curve of the ship's design. When assembled, these sections had a total thickness of four feet four inches.

By the time the *Endurance* set sail on December 17, 1912, it was the strongest wooden ship ever built in Norway. The builders realized that this ship might be the last of its kind. Indeed, it was.

As with Shackleton's other expeditions, his primary head-ache was financing the voyage. He spent almost two years lining up financial backing for the Imperial Trans-Antarctic Expedition, as he had named it. He finally obtained $120,000 from Sir James Caird, a wealthy Scottish jute manufacturer. Parliament offered $50,000, while the Royal Geographical Society contributed a small token of $5,000. Lesser amounts came in from hundreds of interested people all over the world. Shackleton also mortgaged the expedition by selling in advance the rights to whatever commercial assets the expedition might create. He promised to write a book about the trip and sold the rights to the motion pictures and still photographs that would be taken. He also agreed to give a long lecture series on his return. Of course, these arrangements were all made assuming Shackleton would survive.

On the other hand, finding volunteers to take part in the expedition was surprisingly simple. When Shackleton announced his plans, he was flooded by more than 5,000 applications, including three from women. Most of these volunteers were motivated solely by the spirit of adventure. The salaries offered were little more than token payments, ranging from about $240 a year for able seamen to $750 a year for experienced scientists. In most cases, this money was not paid until the end of the expedition anyway. It was considered a privilege to be taken along, and that in itself was payment enough.

Shackleton built his crew around tested veterans. The post of second in command went to his trusted and loyal friend Frank Wild. Thomas Crean—a tall Irishman from the Royal Navy—was assigned to the post of second officer. Crean had served on Scott's Discovery Expedition. Alfred Cheetham, who had already been on three expeditions, including Discovery, was hired as third officer. George Marston came aboard, once again, as the expedition artist. He had done outstanding work for Shackleton's 1907–1909 trek. Another veteran of the *Nimrod*, Thomas McLeod also signed on.

As far as picking newcomers, Shackleton's methods were quite random. If he liked the way a man looked, he was invited. And he made his decision almost immediately. For example, Leonard Hussy was signed on as the meteorologist even though he had practically no qualifications. Shackleton simply thought the man "looked funny." The fact that Hussey had recently returned from an expedition (as an anthropologist) to the sweltering Sudan in Africa also appealed to Shackleton. As part of the deal, Hussey had to take an intensive course in meteorology. Whatever Shackleton's methods were, they seemed to work. He had a great intuition for picking the right men.

During the early months of 1914, Shackleton organized countless supplies of equipment, food stores, and gear that would be needed. This time he opted to take along 69 huskies instead of Manchurian ponies. By the end of July, the *Endurance* was ready for the voyage. On August 1, the ship set sail from London's East India Docks. The trip across the Atlantic took more than two months. During the ocean cruise, the *Endurance* was under the command of Frank Worsley, a New Zealander who had spent 26 years at sea. Shackleton and Wild, who were still tying up loose ends, were to meet up with the rest of the crew at Buenos Aires, Argentina. After a brief stop at Buenos Aires, the *Endurance* set sail on October 26 for her last port of call, the desolate island of South Georgia off the southern tip of South America.

The expedition was finally underway, and there was no going back. For one man on board, this was the moment he'd been waiting for. The crew roster listed 27 men, including Shackleton, but there were 28 men on board. William Bakewell, who had joined the *Endurance* at Buenos Aires, had conspired with Walter How and Thomas McLeod to smuggle aboard his pal, Perce Blackborow. When Blackborow was at last discovered, he was immediately taken before Shackleton. At first, Shackleton was furious. Then, at the height of his tirade, he abruptly stopped. "Finally," Shackleton barked, "if we run out of food and anyone has to be eaten, you will be first. Do you understand?" Blackborow understood that Shackleton was teasing him, and a smile slowly spread across his face. Shackleton then suggested the stowaway help the cook—Charles Green—in the galley.

On November 15, the *Endurance* arrived at the Grytviken whaling station on South Georgia. There, the crew received news that ice conditions in the Weddell Sea—although never good—were the worst they had been in as long as the whalers could remember. Some of them believed it would be impossible for the ship to get through, trying to dissuade Shackleton from trying until the following season. Determined, Shackleton decided to stay at South Georgia for a while in hopes that the situation would improve.

The Weddell Sea was roughly circular in shape, surrounded by three landmasses: the Antarctic continent, the Palmer Peninsula, and the islands of the South Sandwich group. As a result, much of the ice that formed in the Weddell Sea was trapped by the encircling land, which kept it from escaping into the open ocean. In addition, the winds in the area were light compared to Antarctic standards, unable to drive the ice away and even allowing new ice to form in all seasons. Finally, a strong prevailing current flowing in a clockwise direction tended to drive the ice in a huge semicircle, packing it tightly against the Palmer Peninsula on the western side of the sea.

Shackleton's destination was Vahsel Bay, on the opposite shore. There was a sliver of hope that the ice might be carried away from that particular stretch of coast. With some luck, they might be able to slip in behind the worst of the ice along this shore. Shackleton decided to hug the northeast perimeter of the Weddell Sea and its devilish pack, hoping to find the coast along Vahsel Bay ice-free.

On December 5, 1914, the *Endurance* again weighed anchor and pulled out of Cumberland Bay. After two days at sea, the ship passed between Saunders Island in the South Sandwich group and the Candlemas Volcano. There, the men caught the first sight of their enemy—the pack ice. It was only a small patch of light ice, which the ship navigated through without difficulty. Two hours later, however, they came to the back of heavy pack ice several feet thick and half a mile wide. Although they could spot clear water on the other side, heavy waves were rocking the pack. It would have been extremely dangerous to push through.

For several days, they inched along the edge of the pack, searching for a safe opening in the ice. Several times, the *Endurance* smashed into floes head on, but no damage was done. They passed some towering icebergs, some of them more than a square mile, which offered a majestic sight. The water had worn deep ice caverns in many of the bergs, and as each wave crashed into the caverns, a deep, echoing boom resounded. Finally on December 11, they were able to turn south toward Vahsel Bay.

The *Endurance* twisted and wiggled through the pack for nearly two weeks. Movement was stop and go. In open sea, the ship could easily cover 200 miles a day, but in the pack, the ship barely pushed more than 30 miles. Shackleton had hoped they would be ashore by the end of December, but by that time, they had not even crossed the Antarctic Circle. Finally, on January 9, 1915, they rolled into a dark, ice-free ocean that stretched to the horizon. They set a course of south by east and ran at full speed for 100 carefree miles. By midnight the next day, they were 500 feet off a line of 1,000-foot ice cliffs they referred to as "the barrier."

Only 400 miles northeast of Vahsel Bay, the *Endurance* ran parallel with the barrier for five days, making excellent progress. Then, with just 200 miles to go, they sighted heavy pack ice up ahead. Steaming along the edge, Shackleton kept an eye out for a way through. But none could be found. After two days, the ship managed to push into the pack about 10 miles before it was once again cut off. Beyond the heavy pack, Shackleton could see open water. So, he steered the ship into the white-dotted waters.

Almost immediately, the men realized that this ice was very different from anything they had seen before. The floes were thick but soft and consisted mostly of snow. The ship floated in a soupy slush, the mass of ground-up floes closing in on it like pudding around a spoon. First officer Lionel Greenstreet was at the helm. He steered the *Endurance* between two large floes toward a patch of open ocean. Halfway there, the ship got mired in the ice chunks and another floe closed in behind. Even with the engines at full speed, it took two hours to push through. Shackleton decided to let the ship sit for a while to see if the pack would open up.

Six cold, cloudy days went by. By that point, the ice was packed snugly all around the *Endurance*. Unable to move, the men aboard the *Endurance* were forced to wait until the ice broke apart on its own. Still, the ice did not open up. A northerly gale had compressed and crowded the whole Weddell Sea pack against the face of the land. No force on Earth could open up the ice again—except another gale from the opposite direction. It never came. The *Endurance* was frozen tight in the pack, "like an almond in the middle of a chocolate bar," Thomas Orde-Lees, the stores keeper, commented.

Abandon Ship

Over the next few months, the crew made numerous attempts to break the ship free of its ice prison. But each effort ended in failure. Their time eventually ran out. Arctic summer drew to a close, and falling temperatures would keep the ice solid. The drifting pack had carried them to within 60 miles of Vahsel Bay. Although it seemed so close, Shackleton did not want to risk a sledge trip across the ice pack. There was no way they would be able to transport a year's supply of rations and lumber for a hut, especially on sledges drawn by untrained dogs. There was no other choice. They would have to spend their winter on board the ship.

Shackleton was broken. He could have put his party on shore at any of the places they had passed along the barrier. They would at least have been ashore, ready to strike out for the South Pole the following spring. There was no way he could have foreseen these disastrous circumstances yet, he was bitterly disappointed in the way things had played out. The Imperial Trans-Antarctic Expedition's chances of success would be dimished now. Still, he was careful not to reveal his disappointment to the men.

Instead, Shackleton supervised the readying of the ship for the long winter's night ahead. The dogs were moved from the ship to "dogloos" on the floe, and Shackleton organized teams for training the dogs. Everyone was issued warm winter clothing. The officers and scientists moved their equipment and supplies to warmer quarters in the between-deck storage area they decided to call "the Ritz." At once, the men went to work killing a number of seals to build a large supply of meat and blubber. The meat was needed to feed both the crew and the dogs over the winter, and the blubber would be used as fuel to make up for the overuse of coal on the trip south. By April 10, the party had amassed 5,000 pounds of meat and blubber. Shackleton calculated that this amount would last 90 days.

During this time of the year in the Antarctic, the sun does not shine. Although the polar night has been known to drive some men mad, the crew on the *Endurance* kept their spirits up. The winter actually drew them closer together. With little ship work to do, the men found other things to occupy their time. They often gathered in the Ritz to play cards, roll dice, or read. Occasionally, the men entertained one another with skits and lectures. Once a month, Frank Hurley, the photographer, gave a "lantern chat"—a slide show on the places he had visited, including Australia and New Zealand. The favorite show was called "Peeps in Java," which featured palm trees and native maidens.

The mood on the *Endurance* was so light the men sometimes forgot they were frozen in the middle of a drifting floe. Yet, some nights a distant, deep, thundering boom could be heard that would change into a long, creaking groan. It was the sound of pressure—the ice floes pounding and pushing each other.

Suddenly, on July 9, the barometer began to slowly fall. For five consecutive days, the reading slid downward: 29.79 to 29.61 to 29.48 to 29.39 to 29.25. Then, on the morning of July 14, it dropped to 28.88. At seven that night, the snow began to fall. By two the following morning, the whole ship wriggled and shook as the wind tore through the rigging at 70 miles an hour. For the next two days, the temperature continued to drop, at one point to 35°F below zero, and a blizzard raged.

Finally, on July 16, the snow thinned out. Before the storm, the pack had been almost one solid mass of ice. Now it was broken into several large chunks. There was no pressure against the ship at this point. It was stuck in the center of a thick, tough floe. But the eerie booms and whines of pressure could be heard in the distance. Then, the next day, the floe in which the *Endurance* was trapped cracked.

A breakup seemed imminent, and sea watches were kept just in case. Occasionally, a heavy shock traveled through the ice, but still the *Endurance* remained locked in the unbroken center of the floe. The crack froze over again and the watches were temporarily cancelled. Pressure had a power that none of the men had ever witnessed before. One day, Greenstreet went with Wild's dog team for a short run on the floe. Noticing some working ice, they halted to watch. Suddenly, a solid, blue-green floe at least nine feet thick was driven against a neighboring floe. Together, they rose as easily as if they had been two pieces of cork. Back at the ship, Greenstreet recorded the scene in his diary. "Lucky for us if we don't get any pressure like that against the ship," he wrote, "for I doubt whether any ship could stand a pressure that will force blocks like that up."

On August 1, there was a sudden tremble in the floe. The *Endurance* rose upward, with loud scrapes and creaks, then heeled to port and dropped back down into the water. The floe had broken and the ship was loose.

Immediately, Shackleton ran onto the deck, followed by the rest of the crew. As soon as he saw the floe was breaking, he shouted for the men to get the dogs on board. They rushed onto the floe, yanked the chains out of the ice, and hurried the dogs up the gangway. It was just in time. A moment later, the ship rocked violently forward and sideways, pushed up by the ice driving in and under it. The floe battered the side of the ship, knocking the dogloos to pieces against it. The floe continued to batter the ship as the men watched helplessly from the deck. The ordeal continued for 15 agonizing minutes. Then, the *Endurance*'s bow slowly slid up onto the floe ahead, and the pressure subsided. The men breathed a sigh of relief. For the moment, the ship was safe.

Some men felt confident that the *Endurance*, having survived, could stand up to any pressure. But Shackleton was cautious. He told a story about a mouse that lived in a tavern. One night, the mouse found a leaky barrel of beer and drank all he could hold. When he had finished, the mouse sat up and twisted his whiskers. "Now then," he said arrogantly, "where's that [darned] cat?" With his parable, Shackleton was trying to warn the men that being overly confident could get them into a lot of trouble.

Sure enough, the pressure returned on August 29. At midnight, a single strong shock rattled the ship. A moment later, there was a sound like a clap of thunder. Shaken awake, the men sat up in their bunks, waiting for something to happen, but nothing did. The next morning, they noticed a thin crack running out astern, but that was it. The afternoon passed uneventfully. Just as the crew was finishing supper, the *Endurance* shuddered in a second shock. Again, nothing more happened, but the crack astern had widened to a half inch.

The next day passed quietly. At about ten that night, the *Endurance* began moaning like specters in a haunted house. The night watchmen reported that the ice ahead and along the port side was on the move. There was nothing the men could do, so they went to bed. All night long, the ice scraped and battered the hull, making it almost impossible for the crew to sleep. The noise stopped just before dawn but began again late in the afternoon and continued into the evening. By the next afternoon, the pressure again eased. The *Endurance* had survived a second attack.

The rest of September passed without incident. Then, on September 30, the pressure reemerged. It lasted only one terrifying hour. Although some of the decks were permanently buckled, the ship had held strong. Three times the ship had been attacked by the ice, and each time the pressure was greater than the last. Still, the *Endurance* had won the battle. On October 14, the floe that had been jammed under the ship's starboard side since July broke free. For the first time in nine months, the *Endurance* was truly afloat.

From South Georgia
6ᵗʰ DECEMBER 1914

Enters ice pack
(58°-40' S 18° W.)

1000 miles forced through icebergs

WEDDELL

AUGUST 1915
"ENDURANCE"
FLUNG UP
ON ICE
CRUSHED OCT 27ᵗʰ

SIR ERNEST SHACKLETON ATTEMPTS
TO CROSS THE ICE WITH BOATS &
DOG TEAMS. OCT. 30ᵗʰ
BUT RELINQUISHES VENTURE AND
ESTABLISHES "OCEAN CAMP"

On his third voyage to Antarctica, Shackleton and his men became stuck aboard their ship, the *Endurance*, as moving ice floes trapped the vessel in pack ice. As the crew waited for the spring thaw to free the *Endurance*, they realized the shifting ice was instead compressing the wooden boat. Loud cracking and groaning noises forced the crew to abandon the *Endurance* and move their supplies to an ice floe as the boat slowly sank into the water.

Four days later, the floes on either side of the ship closed in and kept pushing together. Several men raced on deck. *Endurance* was being crushed. Everything on the ship not nailed down flew from its place. The *Endurance* was tilted 20 degrees to port, and it continued to roll. Worsley leaned over the rail and watched plank after plank on the side of the ship disappear under the ice.

The floe on the starboard side had got a grip on the bulge of the ship's hull and was simply pushing it over. At 30 degrees, it halted, the lifeboats nearly touching the ice below. As soon as *Endurance* came to rest, everyone went about the job of restoring order, undoubtedly disturbed about what had just happened. Several hours later, the floes drew apart, and the ship righted itself.

In the following days, the crew continued to get ready for when an opening appeared. The engines were still in good working order. Nobody wanted to think about the possibility that the *Endurance*'s luck would eventually run out. On October 25, luck did just that. Shackleton gave the order to abandon ship. The *Endurance* had finally been beaten.

On the Floe

On the floe, the men scrambled to set up a campsite. They crawled in and out of the tents, numbly trying to create some scrap of comfort. Some lined up pieces of lumber to keep their sleeping bags off the snow-covered ice. Others spread pieces of canvas as ground covers. There was not enough flooring for everybody, though, and several men had to sleep on the snow.

Shackleton did not even try to get any sleep. He paced back and forth between the tents, searching his mind for a way to make sense out of what was happening. The pressure was still intense, and several times the campsite shook violently. Two hundred yards away, the black outline of the *Endurance* stood out against the clear night sky. About one in the morning, there was a jolt. Suddenly, a ribbon-like crack snaked across the floe, spreading between some of the tents. At once, it began to widen. Shackleton hurried from tent to tent, waking up the men. It took the better part of an hour in the dark, but they managed to move the camp to the larger half of the floe.

The next morning, the men—stiff and cold from sleeping on the ice—awoke to a dull, overcast sky. The temperature had climbed to 6°F above zero. Shackleton's plan was to march across the floe toward Paulet Island, 346 miles to the northwest, a distance greater than from New York City to Pittsburgh, Pennsylvania. It would be a grueling journey. As the men were packing the sledges, Shackleton called for their attention. He warned them that they must pack light. Each man would be allowed the clothes on his back, two pairs of mittens, six pairs of socks, two pairs of boots, a sleeping bag, a pound of tobacco, and two pounds of personal items. Shackleton pointed out that no item was of any value when weighted against their ultimate survival. When he had finished speaking, he reached under his parka and took out a gold cigarette case and several gold coins and threw them in the snow at his feet. Then, he opened the Bible Queen Alexandra had given him, ripped out the page containing the Twenty-third Psalm and a page from the book of Job. He laid the Bible on the snow and walked away.

The journey began the next day, October 30. They hauled sledges filled with supplies and pulled the lifeboats. Taking the small boats from the sinking ship would be a lifesaving decision. Because of the warm 15-degree temperature, the surface of the ice was soft—far from ideal for sledging. After three hours of lugging the boats and sledges through countless detours, they had only made it one mile. After a week, they had hardly advanced seven miles. Worse, it appeared that they had no safe route to go any farther. To the west, Shackleton saw "a sea of pressure, impossible to advance." He knew the sledges would not last 10 miles over such a surface. Shackleton knew there was only one decision: they would have to stay right where they were until the floe drifted close to land. That is, if it didn't carry them out to sea instead.

They were castaways in one of the most savage regions of the world. They were drifting somewhere, but they did not know where. There was no hope of rescue, and the only food to eat was whatever nature decided to provide. The men made numerous trips back to the original camp, which they named Ocean Camp, for supplies, until the broken ice made it too dangerous to return. The men settled into a humdrum routine that consisted of hunting seals and penguins and basic camp chores. Oddly, most days the men forgot how precarious a situation they were in. Still, Shackleton did not want the men to become too comfortable. Although their floe had remained undamaged by pressure, he did not want a false sense of security to develop. In November, he issued an emergency stations bill. Every man was assigned a specific duty in case the party should suddenly have to strike camp. If their route should be over the ice, the sledge drivers would harness their teams while the other men gathered stores and equipment and took down the tents. If they could escape by water, the men would get the boats ready instead. During the night, the men took turns standing watch in case the floe cracked.

On November 21, the *Endurance* sank. From their camp, the men watched silently as it disappeared beneath the ice. With *Endurance* finally gone, a feeling of complete isolation touched them all. They were alone before, but now in every direction, nothing could be seen but endless ice. Shackleton could not find words to describe the impact of that sight. That night in his diary, he simply stated, "I cannot write about it."

Two months passed, and there was no change in the pack ice. If anything, it was tighter than before. In order to make it to land, they would need a safe opening. The boats could not be used unless the ice opened up. Even if it separated just a little, it was too risky to use the boats. If the floes tightened, the boats would be crushed in an instant.

From January to February, there was a steady southerly gale. During this time, the floe had drifted 68 miles northwest. However, the day-to-day drift was erratic and patternless. Sometimes the floe moved northwest, sometimes due west, straight north, or even south. They were definitely approaching the Palmer Peninsula. But by March, it was still 91 miles away. The men suffered from amenomania—wind madness. Obviously, the disease would only develop in situations like this one—among people marooned on an ice floe, completely dependent on the wind currents for survival. Amenomania exhibits itself in two forms. In one form, a person becomes morbidly anxious about the direction of the wind, gibbering constantly about it. In some cases, people go insane just listening to others obsess about it. The second way it strikes is through the ears. One becomes obsessed with listening for the wind. Most men on the floe experienced both.

With little to do, day in and day out, the men had lots of time to think. Their predicament undoubtedly consumed their thoughts. Surgeon Alexander Macklin wrote in his diary, "I am absolutely obsessed with the idea of escaping. . . . We have been over 4 months on the floe—a time of absolute and utter inutility to anyone. There is absolutely nothing to do but kill time as best one may. . . . One looks forward to meals, not for what one will get, but as definite breaks in the day. All around us we have day after day the same unbroken whiteness, unrelieved by anything at all."

The morning of March 23 dawned with a patchy fog. When Shackleton climbed out of his tent, the fog cleared for a moment and he caught a glimpse of a black object far in the distance to the southwest. He stared at it for a few minutes, then rushed back to his tent and woke his tent mate James Hurley, the photographer. The two men hurried out to the edge of the floe and peered southwest through the narrow strips of broken fog. Shackleton wasn't imagining things. It was there—land.

"Land in sight! Land in sight!" Shackleton shouted as he ran back to camp. The island was one of the tiny Danger Islets, its tabletop bluffs rising steeply out of the water. It was 42 miles away. Twenty miles beyond that was Paulet Island. If the pack would open, the men could land in a day. But no one believed the pack would open. The men could count 70 icebergs around them. For the moment, they seemed to be preventing the pack from either opening up or drifting much to the north. If they launched the boats, they would be crushed within minutes. Instead of exciting them, the sight of land only reminded them of their helplessness. All they could do was wait for the ice to open. Still, the ice would not let them loose, and they continued to drift.

In the early morning of March 29, the night watchman—third officer Alfred Cheetham—dashed among the tents. "Crack!" he shouted. "Crack! Lash up and stow!" The floe had split in two places, one running the length of the floe and another snaked at right angles to the first. The men ran to one of the boats—the *James Caird*—to rescue it from being lost in the crack. Soon, the center crack widened out to 20 feet in some places. The store of meat was on the opposite side, so several men jumped across and quickly tossed the meat over the open water to the other side.

The floe was heaving with the swell—waves created by open sea. The swell raised the men's hopes that the ice might be opening up. Plus, Worsley sighted a giant petrel—a snow-white bird, except for two black stripes across its wings—a definite sign of open water. The biologist, Robert Clark, spotted a jellyfish in one of the cracks and stated that such creatures were only found in ice-free seas. "It certainly looks promising," Worsley commented. But then he added, "Hope tells a flattering tale."

Once a mile in diameter, their floe was now less than 200 yards across. Most of the time it was surrounded by open water, constantly tossed by swells and collision with other floes. Clarence Island, the easternmost of the South Shetland Islands north of the Antarctic Peninsula, was 68 miles due north, and they appeared to be drifting toward it. But a gradual westerly drift threatened to sweep them out to sea through Loper Channel—the 80-mile-wide gulf between Elephant Island (the northernmost of the South Shetland Islands) and King George Island (the largest of the South Shetland Islands located close to the northern tip of the Antarctic Peninsula).

By April 8, it looked as if their worst fears were coming true. The floe was drifting straight for the open sea. They would have to reach Clarence Island or Elephant Island. From the floe, they could see the mountain peaks on each of them. If the winds did not change, they might miss their last chance at land. During the day, the ice floes began drifting apart from one another. By the next morning, though, the ice had closed again. Again, during the day, open water spread through the pack.

Suddenly, the floe cracked and split in two. Once again, the men scrambled to save their boats and provisions. The two halves rapidly pulled apart. Before long, there would be nothing left of their floe. Shackleton was torn. Should he launch the boats regardless of the risk? The floes might suddenly close on them. Yet, if they stayed at the camp, they might not get another chance at survival. For the moment, the pack was open. Finally, Shackleton gave the orders, "Launch the boats."

After five and a half months on the floe, no one was sorry to get off. By early afternoon, the three boats—the *James Caird*, the *Stancomb Wills*, and the *Dudley Docker*—were in open water. The men had little time to take one last look as they drew away from the ice floe they had come to know as Patience Camp. They were barely in the water, and the ice began to close.

Impossible
Rescue

THE POSITION FROM WHICH THE BOATS WERE LAUNCHED was 61°56'S, 53°56'W, near the eastern edge of what is now Bransfield Strait. About 200 miles long and 60 miles wide, the Bransfield Strait lies between the Palmer Peninsula and the South Shetland Islands. This area of water connects the hazardous Drake Passage with the Weddell Sea. These waters are treacherous, especially for small sailing boats. Today, the U.S. Navy Department describes the conditions of the Bransfield Strait as strong, erratic currents, sometimes reaching a velocity of six knots. The currents are affected only slightly by the wind, so an effect known to sailors as a "cross sea" is set up. A cross sea happens when the wind is blowing in one direction and the current moves in another. During a cross sea, waves of water as tall as 10 feet are heaved upward, making a perilous journey for a small boat.

On the afternoon of April 9, 1916, Shackleton and his men faced angry waters. As they threaded their boats through the chunks of ice, they suddenly heard a deep, hoarse noise rapidly growing louder. Looking to the starboard side, they saw a lava-like river of churning, tumbling ice about two feet high bearing down on them. Shackleton recognized it as a tide rip, a current thrown up from the ocean floor that had caught a mass of ice and was heading straight for the boats at about three knots.

For a moment, the men just stared in disbelief. Then Shackleton swung the bow of the *James Caird* to port and shouted at the others to do the same with the other two boats. Immediately, the oarsmen pulled away from the onrushing ice. Even rowing with all their strength, the tide was gaining on them. The *Dudley Docker* was the most cumbersome boat to row, and twice it almost capsized, but the men managed to keep it afloat. Just about the time the oarsmen could row no more, the tide rip began to flatten out, and it disappeared as mysteriously as it had risen.

Shackleton commanded the *James Caird*, the most sea-worthy of the three boats. Designed to Worsley's specifications, it was a double-ended whaleboat, 22 feet six inches long. The *Dudley Docker* (steered by Worsley) and the *Stancomb Wills* (steered by navigator Hubert Hudson) were cutters—heavy, square-sterned boats of solid oak. They were 21 feet nine inches long, designed as pulling boats—not for rowing or sailing. In terms of men, the boats were not overloaded. The *Wills* carried eight men, the *Docker* nine, and the *Caird* eleven. With less bulky gear, each boat could have accommodated at least twice that number. However, with supplies and sleeping bags crammed into each vessel, the men barely had room to stretch their legs, much less curl up for some much-needed sleep.

They rowed all afternoon until about five thirty. The three boats had made excellent progress. As night moved in, they found a flat, heavy floe about 200 yards across. Shackleton decided it would be sturdy enough for them to camp on for the night. The party pitched the tents, ate supper, and turned in. About eleven o'clock, Shackleton felt strangely uneasy, so

As the ice floes began to break apart and separate, floating into open water, the men of the *Endurance* expedition realized they had to leave their drifting camp and find land. Shackleton and his crew used three lifeboats—the *James Caird*, the *Stancomb Wills*, and the *Dudley Docker*—to transport themselves and their supplies to the safety of Elephant Island.

he dressed and went outside. He noticed that the swell had increased, spinning the floe around and carrying it out to sea. A few minutes later, he heard a deep thud, and the floe split right beneath his feet—directly under one of the tents where eight men were sleeping peacefully. Almost instantly, the two pieces of the floe pulled apart. The tent collapsed, followed by a splash.

"Somebody's missing," one man shouted. Shackleton rushed over and tore the tent away. In the dark, he could see a shapeless form wriggling in the water—a man in a sleeping bag.

Shackleton reached down and pulled the man, Ernie Holness, out of the water. A moment later, the two halves of the broken floe smashed together. He was soaking wet and cold but alive. Then, all of a sudden, the crack opened again, separating the party on the different floes. The men on one side tossed a line across, and the two groups of men pulled toward one another. They managed to bring the halves together again. They hurriedly moved everything over to one floe. Afterward, one by one, the men leaped over the crack to the other side. Shackleton waited until everyone was safely across. By the time it was his turn, the pieces had drifted apart too far for him to make the jump. Quickly, he snatched up the rope and tried to pull his floe closer, but it was no use. Without the others, he was not strong enough to move it. Minutes later his floe drifted away and he disappeared into the darkness.

From somewhere, the men heard Shackleton's voice call, "Launch a boat." They slid the *Wills* into the water, and half a dozen volunteers scrambled on board. Rowing toward Shackleton's voice, they managed to find their commander and bring him back to the floe. Back with the rest of the party, Shackleton checked on Holness. He was shivering uncontrollably in his sopping clothes, but there were no dry garments to give him. So, Shackleton ordered that he be kept moving until his clothes dried out. For the rest of the night, his companions took turns walking Holness up and down the floe, his frozen clothes cracking with each step. Holness did not complain about his clothes, but he grumbled for hours that he had lost his tobacco in the water.

The next morning, the boats were launched again. After another day of rowing, the men began searching for a place to camp for the night. They spotted a "floe-berg," a thick mass of dark-blue pressure ice about 35 yards square, which in some places rose 15 feet above the water. Shackleton reluctantly gave the order to camp on the ice. He knew that icebergs of any sort were unpredictable. A sudden shift could overturn them. But the men needed sleep, and the water was too rough for them to get any in the boats.

During the night, the wind rose to almost gale force. The winds drove great quantities of ice around the floe-berg. By morning, the pack extended unbroken to the horizon in every direction. Berg fragments and shattered floes in thousands of different shapes littered the surface of the water. The pack pounded their floe-berg on every side while the surge of the swell ate away at the ice at the waterline. From time to time, chunks dropped off here and there, torn loose by the floes banging against the berg. The berg was crumbling beneath them. At any moment, it might split or upend. Yet, they could not launch the boats. They would have been crushed to splinters in a matter of minutes.

They waited all afternoon for a break in the pack, while the berg was being destroyed on all sides. Suddenly, just before two o'clock, a pool of water opened up. The ice seemed to be mysteriously pulling away from the open water, as if some invisible force was clearing a path. "Launch the boats!" Shackleton shouted. The men shoved the boats into the water and pushed away. Once again, they had narrowly escaped death.

After seven days and seven nights in open boats, the men at last caught sight of land. The outline of Elephant Island popped out of a gray sky less than 15 miles away. Finally, relief was within reach. They had gone almost 80 hours since their last sleep. Their bodies were drained, and exposure to the wind and freezing water sloshing around at their feet had taken a devastating toll on them as well. Several of the men suffered from serious frostbite.

Early that afternoon, the 3,500-foot peaks of Elephant Island rose steeply out of the sea ahead. The men figured they were probably no more than 10 miles off, but after an hour of rowing toward it, the island was still the same distance away.

The wind had shifted to the north so that they were working against it practically still.

Shackleton thought it might increase their speed if they tied the boats together, one behind the other, with the *Docker* in the lead. It didn't help. Around five in the evening, the wind died down. They took to the oars with all their might. Half an hour later, the wind suddenly picked up again, blowing nearly 50 miles an hour. Shackleton decided to separate the boats. They kept pushing toward Elephant Island, battling the wind and the ocean spray, making little headway.

About midnight, Shackleton looked over and noticed that the *Docker* was gone. Quickly, he ordered the candle in the compass binnacle lighted and then hoisted it up the mast so that it shone on the *Caird*'s sail. No answering light flickered in the distance. Shackleton instructed Hussey to light a match every few minutes and hold it up so that it flared against the white of the sail. One after another, Hussey struck the matches while Shackleton kept his eyes focused into the darkness. Still, there was no sign of the lost *Docker*.

What Shackleton did not know was that the *Docker* had tried to answer his call. Only half a mile away, the men had seen the *Caird*'s signal in the dark. In response, they lit their only candle under a tent cloth, but the flame was not bright enough for Shackleton to see. At the *Caird*, Shackleton's attention was ripped away from his lost men when a violent tide rip wildly pitched the boat.

All the boats—even the missing *Docker*—struggled to fight the heaving waves. Having been at the oars all day, the men were on the brink of exhaustion. Gradually, a pale hint of light spread across the eastern horizon. Over the course of the night, the men had lost their bearings. Silently, each one prepared himself for the shock of seeing an empty sea or, at best, the distant outline of an island too far away to reach. As the sky slowly brightened, the enormous gray cliffs of Elephant Island came into view dead ahead. Land was only a few hundred yards away.

On the *Caird*, Shackleton still caught no sight of the *Docker*, which rocked in the waves on the other side of a cliff. His anxiety had been mounting all night. He was responsible for the lives of his men. Although he had tremendous faith in Worsley's seamanship, the night had demanded much more than skill. He feared the men aboard the *Docker* had perished during the night. Likewise, on the *Docker*, Worsley and the others believed they alone had survived. Then, just as the *Docker* rounded a tiny chunk of land, the masts of the *Caird* and the *Wills* appeared in the distance. Later that morning, the three reunited boats rested on the shores of Elephant Island. They had spent seven days and nights wrestling with the open boats. Several men collapsed on the beach, unable to walk on their frostbitten feet. But they were on land—for the first time in 497 days.

Across South Georgia

Shackleton and his men had found land, but they were far from rescue. Elephant Island was a desolate strip of land, void of towns or people. On April 20, Shackleton announced his plans for rescue. He would take a party of five men and sail in the *Caird*—the most seaworthy vessel—for South Georgia. There, he could get a ship and return to Elephant Island for the others. The news came as no surprise to the men. However, they also realized that Shackleton's chances of actually reaching South Georgia were small. The boat party would have to travel more than 800 miles across the stormiest ocean in the world. Their ultimate goal was to reach an island no more than 25 miles wide at its widest spot. To guide an open boat that distance, under harsh conditions, would be a frighteningly difficult task. Then, to strike such a pinpoint on the map would dramatically test even Worsley's skill as a navigator. Besides Worsley—who would be indispensible in these circumstances—Shackleton

After a harrowing experience traveling from ice floe to Elephant Island (*above*) in three open lifeboats, Shackleton chose five crew members to accompany him in search of rescue. The six sailors launched the *James Caird* into one of the most tumultuous seas in the world, hoping to reach South Georgia for help.

chose to take second officer Thomas Crean, carpenter Harry McNeish, and two of the most able seamen—John Vincent and Timothy McCarthy.

Shackleton was careful and selective in his choices. Crean was a tough, tested sailor who followed orders without question. Shackleton was confident that Crean's rough, determined nature would weather the challenges. Fifty-seven years old, McNeish was probably not up to the journey physically. But both Shackleton and Wild saw him as a potential troublemaker and, therefore, not a good man to leave behind. Also, if the *James Caird* was to become damaged by ice—a distinct possibility—McNeish's expertise would be invaluable. Although he was much like McNeish in personality, Vincent had brute strength on his side. Likewise, Shackleton chose McCarthy because he was built like a bull. This adventure would push their endurance to the limit. As for those left behind, Shackleton put their lives in the hands of his most trusted colleague and friend—Frank Wild.

Before he set out, Shackleton spent almost the entire night talking with Wild. He instructed him on many different subjects, ranging from what should be done if the rescue party failed to the distribution of tobacco.

On April 24, 1914, the *James Caird* was positioned offshore—sails set and loaded with enough stores to last a month. Handshakes and good wishes exchanged, the rescue party hoisted the sails and waved one last goodbye to their pals. "The men who were staying behind made a pathetic little group on the beach," observed Shackleton, "with the grim heights of the island behind them and the sea seething at their feet, but they waved to us and gave us their hearty cheers." On shore, the castaways watched the *James Caird* fade out of sight, which did not take long for such a tiny boat on the great, heaving ocean.

To make the ship more seaworthy, McNeish had attached a piece of canvas across the top. Below this decking, the men could cook meals and find some relief from the wind and icy ocean spray. They took two-hour shifts at the tiller. The men who were not on watch crawled into the wet sleeping bags and tried to get some rest. Try as they might, there was no comfort in the boat. They were cramped in narrow quarters, continuously doused with the spray and cold. Daily they fought the sea and winds. Almost always there were gales, and they quickly realized the weakness of their decking. The continuous blows shifted the weight of anything tied above the canvas—the boxes of store and sledge-runners. Before long, the canvas began to sag and accumulate water. With each rocking wave, icy trickles of ocean water poured through the canvas opening into the boat. The men took turns bailing out buckets of water, trying to keep things dry, which was virtually impossible.

On April 28, four days and 150 miles out from Elephant Island, a raw and penetrating rain began to fall. The wind picked up from the north, blowing against them. They had entered the zone where they might encounter ice, and there was no time to spare. They could not risk being blown a single mile south. The struggle began to hold the boat steady. All day, the men took a wearisome pounding from the rain. The temperature dropped, and the spray froze on the boat and decking, dangerously reducing the buoyancy of the boat. They could not let the load of ice keep building, so they crawled out onto the decking, chipping and picking the ice away as the angry waves tossed the little ship from side to side.

By the next morning, the wind had eased, but the boat was in a perilous situation. The *Caird* was not rising to the oncoming seas. The weight of the ice was dragging it down like a log. Immediately, the men sprang into action, tossing overboard anything they could get rid of, hoping to lighten the *Caird*'s load. They broke away the spare oars, which were encased in ice and frozen to the sides of the boat, and threw them overboard. They pitched two of their six sleeping bags, each weighing about 40 pounds. They also attacked the boat with any tool they had, chipping and scraping away as much ice as they could.

The boat was not the only thing deteriorating. All of the men complained about a feeling of tightness in their feet and legs. When McNeish took off his boots, his legs, ankles, and feet were puffy and dead white. The rest of the men decided to check their feet as well. Frostbite covered any bare flesh, causing large blisters on their fingers and hands. Somehow, they managed to endure their stinging pain enough to bring the ship through the various gales. By the seventh day, they had covered 380 miles. They had made it almost halfway to South Georgia. "It looked as if we were going to get through," Shackleton later wrote in *South*, his account of the expedition.

At midnight on May 6, day 12, Shackleton was at the tiller when he suddenly noticed a line of clear sky between the south and the southwest. The sky was overcast and occasional snow squalls had added to a tremendous cross sea. But Shackleton thought the sky was finally clearing. A moment later, he realized that what he had seen was not a break in the clouds but the white crest of an enormous wave. "During twenty-six years' experience of the ocean in all its moods I had never seen a wave so gigantic," he wrote. He shouted to the other men, "For God's sake, hold on! It's got us!"

The men felt the boat lifted and flung forward. The heaving and churning waves tossed the *Caird* like a toy. Somehow, the boat stayed afloat—although half filled with water and sagging from the weight. The men mustered every ounce of energy and bailed like they had never bailed before, flinging the water over the sides with any receptacle they could find. Miraculously, the wave passed, and the *Caird* was still afloat.

Shortly after noon on May 8, the men caught sight of the black cliffs of South Georgia. They had sailed from Elephant Island 14 days earlier on a mission that seemed impossible. Unbelievably, they had prevailed. But the final stage of their journey was yet to come—a march across South Georgia.

By sea, the rescue party was still about 150 miles away from their destination, Stromness Whaling Station on the other side of the island. McNeish and Vincent had suffered terribly from the boat journey. Shackleton doubted they could handle another 150 miles by sea. The other alternative was to attempt the crossing by land. Although it was a mere 29 miles in a straight line, no one had ever before crossed South Georgia. To make matters more grim, no one believed it could be done.

A few of the peaks on South Georgia rise to less than 10,000 feet—certainly not high by mountain-climbing standards. However, the interior of the island has been described as "a saw-tooth thrust through the tortured upheaval of mountain and glacier that falls in chaos to the northern sea." In other words, to most it was impassable. Shackleton knew this, but he had no choice. He would have to attempt another impossible journey in order to rescue his men marooned on Elephant Island.

Shackleton decided to take Worsley and Crean with him and leave McCarthy, McNeish, and Vincent behind at camp on the north side of King Haakon Bay. The route of the overland party would start out toward the seaward end of the glacier on the east side of the camp. They would then travel up a snow slope which seemed to lead to a pass in the great Allardyce Range, which forms the backbone of South Georgia and dips into a well-defined pass from east to west. Shackleton planned to climb the pass and head eastward to Stromness Bay.

The men overhauled their gear. Shackleton realized the sledge would be too heavy and cumbersome to pull through the snow plains, glaciers, and peaks. They also decided to leave the sleeping bags behind to make a lighter march. They packed three days' provisions, a lamp filled with oil, the small cooker, an ice axe, and a 50-foot rope for lowering themselves down steep slopes or across crevassed glaciers. They had no skis or snowshoes, so they would have to make the march in the worn boots on their feet. They set out on Friday, May 19.

By the second day, the men had made it to the razorback of the Allardyce Range. Shackleton looked out in disappointment. In front of him was a sheer cliff that fell to a bed of crumpled ice 1,500 feet below. There was no way down. To the east, he saw a vast snow upland, sloping upward for seven or eight miles to a height of at least 4,000 feet. On the north side, the land fell away into steep glaciers, and to the south the terrain was broken by huge outfalls. He decided that their path would have to be between the glaciers and the outfalls. But first, they would have to descend from the ridge on which they were standing. They had to retrace their steps back down and head to the northeast.

As they skirted the base of the mountain, they came to a gigantic gully, a mile and a half long and 1,000 feet deep. They passed through it, but on the other side they came to another sharp drop. The hot sun had loosened the snow, making the march treacherous. Looking back, they could see a fog was rolling up behind them. They had to get down to the lower areas before they were enveloped in the fog. Realizing how important it was to get down into the next valley, Shackleton turned to his companions. He unroped and sat down in the snow. The other two followed his lead. "Come on boys," he said. And they slid off down the slope, as if they were kids enjoying an afternoon on their toboggans.

They could not see the bottom, and there was the possibility that the slope ended abruptly in a steep drop. But it was too late to turn back now. They finally slowed to a stop at the foot of the slope, after sliding at least 900 feet in a couple of minutes. The men turned back to see the gray fingers of the fog clawing at the ridge. They had escaped.

Instead of stopping to camp, they decided to keep moving. Darkness fell, and the full moon rose in the sky, casting a silver pathway for their feet. They were on their way up again, and by midnight, they were again at an elevation of 4,000 feet. They continued to follow the light, using the moon to guide them northeast. By early morning, they felt almost sure they were above Stromness Bay.

Their high hopes were suddenly dashed. They spotted crevasses, revealing that they were on another glacier. Shackleton knew there was no glacier in Stromness and figured they must be at Fortuna Glacier. They were still a good deal away from their destination.

Eventually, they made it to the jagged line of peaks near Fortuna Bay. Their route to Stromness lay across it. They climbed a steep slope up to the ridge and leaned into the icy wind as they passed through the mountain gap. Then they caught a glimpse of the twisted, wavelike rock formations of Husvik Harbor, near Stromness. The journey seemed to be almost over. "Boss, it looks too good to be true!" Worsley said. But they still had 12 miles of rugged country to cross.

On May 20, the men climbed a final ridge. Below, they saw a little steamer—a whaling boat—entering the bay 2,500 feet below. The tiny moving figures below meant they were no longer alone. With handshakes and pats on the back, the men cautiously started down the slope to civilization. Their pathway was a channel cut by water running from upland. They followed the course of the stream, through the icy water, wet to the waist and shivering. Suddenly they heard a familiar sound which brought with it a rush of terror. They had come to the top of a waterfall, with a drop of 25 or 30 feet. In their weary condition—after hiking for nearly 36 hours—there was no way they could turn and climb back up the channel. They would have to go down the waterfall.

With some difficulty, they managed to tie one end of the rope to a boulder. Then, Shackleton and Worsley lowered Crean, the heaviest man. He disappeared in the tumbling water and came out gasping at the bottom. Shackleton went next, followed by Worsley, sliding down the rope into the freezing water below. Shivering, they hurried toward the whaling station, not more than half a mile away. When they got to the wharf, Shackleton asked the man in charge if Mr. Sorlle—the manager—was in the house.

The man then disappeared in the manager's house. "There are three funny-looking men outside, who say they have come over the island and they know you," the man told Sorlle. Seventeen months earlier, when Shackleton had docked in South Georgia, he had met Sorlle. At once, Sorlle got up and went to the door. "Well?" he said to the men standing outside.

"Don't you know me?" Shackleton asked.

"I know your voice," Sorlle replied. "You're the mate of the *Daisy*."

"My name is Shackleton," he said.

Immediately, Sorlle swung open the door. "Come in. Come in," he exclaimed.

Shackleton hesitated and looked at his friends. "I'm afraid we smell," he said. Sorlle chuckled and reminded them that they were at a whaling station.

Inside, Shackleton and the others enjoyed a warm bath, a shave, and a hearty meal. Immediately after dinner, Worsley went aboard the whaler *Samson* for the trip around South Georgia to the place were McNeish, McCarthy, and Vincent were camped. The *Samson* arrived at King Haakon Bay the following morning. For a moment, the three men waiting there did not recognize Worsley because of his cleanshaven face. They all arrived back at Stromness station the next day—May 22. They even brought the *Caird*, which by this time was more like a dear companion than a boat.

Meanwhile, Shackleton refused to get too comfortable. He still had men to rescue. He arranged with the Chilean government for the use of a large tugboat called the *Yelcho* in which to return to Elephant Island to rescue the rest of his men. On the morning of May 23, 1916, less than 72 hours after arriving at Stromness, Shackleton and his two companions set out for Elephant Island.

Once again, the pack ice tried to stop Shackleton, but he refused to give up. After 100 days, and three failed attempts, Shackleton finally spotted the coast of Elephant Island on August 30.

Return to Elephant Island

Meanwhile on Elephant Island, the 22 castaways had been battling blizzards, frostbite, and dwindling stores. Shackleton and the others had been gone for more than four months. The men assumed their leader had perished on the way to South

ROSS SEA PARTY

The Ross Sea party was a crucial part of Shackleton's Imperial Trans-Antarctic Expedition. Shackleton's plan was to land with his group from the *Endurance* on the coast of Antarctica throughtout the Weddell Sea, and then march across the continent to McMurdo Sound on Ross Island. Because Shackleton and his men could not carry the needed provisions for the entire course of the expedition, another ship, the *Aurora*, and a crew were sent to establish a base at McMurdo Sound. From a base there, this party would lay a series of depots across the Great Ice Barrier to the South Pole. The survival of Shackleton's party would absolutely depend on these depots being laid. Meanwhile, as the second party built depots, the *Aurora* would remain moored in the sound to wait for Shackleton's party on completion of their mission.

Unaware of the fate of the *Endurance*, the Ross Sea party continued their mission, depositing food supplies for Shackleton's team, who would never show up. From the start, things went wrong, including the party's lack of confidence in its captain, Eneas Mackintosh. While a party of 10 men was out laying depots the ice floe holding the *Aurora* broke free and carried it out to sea. It began a long drift northward away from Cape Evans, out of McMurdo Sound, into the Ross Sea. On February 12, 1916, the ship at last broke from the ice floe and reached New Zealand on April 2.

The loss of the ship created an overwhelming obstacle for the expedition. Most of the shore party's personal items,

(Continues)

(Continued)

food, equipment, and fuel was still on the *Aurora*, leaving ten men stranded on shore with nothing but the clothes on their backs. To make matters worse, the men had no idea what had happened to the ship and when, if ever, it might return. Luckily, they were able to move into the hut that had been built and abandoned by Robert Scott just before he died. This shelter provided ample clothing, footwear, and equipment.

Convinced that Shackleton would finish his crossing in a few months, the men resumed their work of laying depots. They continued to experience epic misfortune and hardships. Some of the men developed scurvy and snow blindness in the extreme weather, and their supplies ran out. The party lost three of its men—one to scurvy and exhaustion; two disappeared into a blizzard, with only their tracks found leading to the edge of broken ice.

After two years, the men were scared and desperate. They could not imagine surviving another winter. Then the impossible happened. On August 31, 1916, after two years of silence, Shackleton miraculously reappeared. Seeing him emerge from the rescue ship instead of from Beardmore Glacier meant that all their work had been in vain. Although the Ross Sea party actually completed its task, it was Shackleton's story of failure that became famous. In general, when comparing Shackleton's remarkable endurance to the amazing survival of the *Aurora* crew, it is clear that the accomplishments of the Ross Sea Party has been overshadowed by their expedition leader. They have been referred to as "Shackleton's Forgotten Men."

Georgia. Even if he had made it, some days the pack ice stretched all the way to the horizon. No one believed Shackleton could get a rescue ship through it. "Some of the party have quite given up all hope of [a ship] coming," Dr. Alexander Macklin wrote in his diary. On August 19, Orde-Lees wrote, "There is no good in deceiving ourselves any longer."

Still, Wild tried to keep hope alive. "Lash up and stow boys," he would say each day. "The Boss may come today."

At first, August 30 seemed to be like any other day. Someone would climb the bluff and search the sea for some speck of a ship. That day, however, he would not return to the hut in disappointment. Expedition artist George Marston had lingered atop the bluff to do some sketching. Suddenly, he came dashing back down the trail. He burst into the hut and exclaimed, "There's a boat. Shall we light a fire?"

For an instant, the men were so stunned they could not move. Then they exploded into a tumbling stampede. They were so excited, some of them tore down the canvas walls to see the unbelievable truth. They all ran to the beach, some without their boots on. "We tried to cheer," wrote Hussey, "but excitement gripped our vocal cords."

When the boat got near enough, the men on the beach heard the familiar voice of their commander. "Are you all right?" he shouted.

"All safe, all well," they yelled back. A smile of relief spread across Shackleton's face. "Thank God," he said. At last, after 137 days stranded at Elephant Island, they were rescued.

The *Quest*

SHACKLETON REACHED NEW ZEALAND AT THE BEGINNING OF December 1916. There he found that arrangements for the rescue of the Ross Sea party were complete. Before Shackleton had gotten in touch with the outside world, the New Zealand government had handled the relief task. The governments of Great Britain and Australia were also providing financial assistance for the rescue. The *Aurora* had been repaired and refitted at Port Chalmers during the year, and it was ready for the voyage back to McMurdo Sound.

Captain John Davis, a member of Shackleton's Antarctic Expedition in 1907-1909 had been placed in command of *Aurora* by the governments, and he had hired officers, engineers, and crew. At Shackleton's arrival in New Zealand, Davis at once went to see him. He gave Shackleton the full account of his voyage and drift in the *Aurora*. Captain Davis was ready to take the ship to McMurdo Sound, and Shackleton went along to take charge of any necessary shore operations.

On December 20, 1916, the *Aurora* set sail from Port Chalmers. After a quick passage, the ship pulled up alongside the ice-covered edge of Cape Royds on January 10, 1917. Shackleton went ashore with a party to look for some record of the survivors in the hut that he had used in the Nimrod Expedition. There he found a letter revealing that the Ross Sea party had been seen coming from Cape Evans. That afternoon, seven survivors of the Ross Sea party boarded *Aurora*. The survivors told Shackleton that Eneas Mackintosh (the commander), Reverend Arnold Spencer-Smith, and Victor Hayward had died. Although all well, the survivors showed traces of exhaustion and stress from the ordeal they had just overcome.

Shackleton decided they should make a final search for the bodies of Mackintosh and Hayward. According to Joyce, they had already searched the area south of Glacier Tongue. Shackleton planned to search the area north of that point, as well as the old depot off Butter Point. On January 12, the ship stopped at a point five and a half miles east of Butter Point. Shackleton led a party across the water-logged ice to within 30 yards of the spot, but because of the high cliffs and loose, slushy ice, they could not reach it. There was no sign of the depot or anyone having visited the area, so they abandoned their search. Shackleton and the party returned to the ship and headed across the Sound to Cape Bernacchi.

The next day, Shackleton again took the party ashore to search the area north of Glacier Tongue. On January 15, a blizzard stopped them from sledging, so they spent the day organizing the hut at Cape Evans. The following morning, Shackleton and Joyce went to Glacier Tongue. From the top, they could see that there was no chance of finding any remains. The enormous snowdrifts from the blizzard rose 10 to 15 feet high. They decided to give up the search. While they were out searching, Wild and Jack erected a cross to the memory of their three lost comrades. The *Aurora* turned north to New Zealand, arriving at last on February 9. The expedition had finally drawn to a close.

Gone Home

After the rescue of the Ross Sea party, Shackleton spent some time in Australia and on a lecture tour in the United States before returning home. On May 29, 1917, he landed back in England and was reunited with Emily and his three children: Raymond, Cecily, and Edward. Shackleton was anxious to play some part in World War I, but nothing suitable could be found for him. He made the acquaintance of Sir Edward Carson, the famous Anglo-Irish politician. Carson sent Shackleton to South America to improve British propaganda techniques. In April 1918, Shackleton returned to England.

By 1920, Shackleton was longing to return again to the polar regions. This frost-covered continent felt more like his home than any other place on Earth. "Sometimes I think I am no good at anything but being away in the wilds," he once said. An old school friend agreed to finance another expedition. By the time the offer came, though, Shackleton had only three months to plan and outfit the expedition, half the time it had taken him for both the *Nimrod* and the *Endurance*. This time, the expedition's plans were somewhat vague—to circumnavigate the Antarctic continent or perhaps search for an uncharted isle or Captain Kidd's treasure. He talked about mapping the unknown Enderby Quadrant of Antarctica. More than anything, though, he wanted to be at sea with his crew again, to survive the outlandish, discover the unknown, and walk where no man had walked before.

His crew set sail aboard the *Quest* on September 17, 1921. Its captain was none other than Frank Wild. Some of the other crewmen from the *Endurance* also signed up for the expedition, including Worsley, Macklin, McIlroy, Hussey, Kerr, Green, Scot, and McLeod. In Rio de Janeiro, Brazil,

Shackleton, never completely comfortable on dry land and around familiar territory, longed once again to return to Antarctica on another exploration. Setting off on the *Quest* with some of his former crewmates of the *Endurance*, it was Shackleton's last voyage and adventure.

Shackleton suffered a heart attack but refused to be examined. His old friends saw signs that their commander was not himself. Shackleton even admitted in his diary, "I grow old and tired but must always lead on." As the *Quest* passed its first iceberg, though, Shackleton felt perfectly at ease. "The old familiar sight aroused in me memories that the strenuous year had deadened," he wrote. "When things are going well I wonder what internal difficulty will be sprung on me."

The next day, January 4, 1922, the peaks of South Georgia Island broke the horizon. Shackleton and Worsley scurried on deck "like a pair of excitable kids," Worsley wrote. They pointed out to each other those familiar landmarks from not so long ago—Fortuna Bay and the steep snow slope that they had slid down. Suddenly, the boss seemed more like the old Shackleton.

"When I look back on those days I have no doubt that Providence guided us," Shackleton wrote in *South*, "not only across those snow fields, but across the storm-white sea that separated Elephant Island from our landing-place on South Georgia. I know that during that long and racking march of 36 hours over the unnamed mountains and glaciers of South Georgia, it seemed to me that we were four, not three. I said nothing to my companions on the point, but afterwards Worsley said to me, 'Boss, I had a curious feeling on the march that there was another person with us.' Crean confessed to the same idea."

In South Georgia late that night, Shackleton looked tired. Just before three in the morning, he suffered another heart attack. He called out to Macklin, who rushed to his bedside. Macklin tucked a blanket around his leader, lecturing him about how he should change his habits—watch his diet, get more sleep. "You're always wanting me to give up things," Shackleton said. "What is it I ought to give up?" A few minutes later, on January 5, 1922, Ernest Shackleton gave up his life. He was 47 years old.

Shortly after dawn, Wild called all hands on deck and gave them the devastating news. Then he announced that the expedition would carry on. Shackleton's death shocked everyone, even those who knew he wasn't feeling well. After all he had lived through, he seemed indestructible. "Now that he is gone," Hussey wrote, "there is a gap in our lives that can never be filled."

A friend remembered that Shackleton had wanted to die on one of his expeditions, far away from England. "I shall be going, old man," Shackleton told him, "till one day I shall not come back." Knowing this, Emily instructed that her husband be buried in South Georgia. The Farthest South had always been his true love. On March 5, 1922, his body was laid to rest in a small cemetery in Grytviken. His funeral was attended by the most important people in Shackleton's life: the hardworking, hardhanded sailors and whaling captains of the polar regions.

CHRONOLOGY

1874   Ernest Henry Shackleton born in county Kildare,
        Ireland, on February 15.

1890   Leaves Dulwich College at age 16 and goes to sea.

1901   Joins the National Antarctic Expedition
        commanded by Robert Falcon Scott and sets sail
        on the *Discovery*.

1902   Together with Scott and Wilson, gets closer to the South
        Pole than anyone before on December 30.

TIMELINE

With Scott and Wilson, gets
closer to the South Pole than
anyone before on December 30

1874   **1901**   **1909**

1902

Born in county Kildare,
Ireland, on February 15

Joins the National Antarctic
Expedition commanded by
Robert Falcon Scott and sets
sail on the *Discovery*

Gets within 97 miles of the
South Pole;

1904   Marries Emily Dorman on April 8; over their years together, the couple have three children—Raymond, Cecily, and Edward.

1909   With three other men, gets within 97 miles of the South Pole; knighted Sir Ernest Shackleton.

1911   Norwegian Roald Amundsen becomes the first person to reach the South Pole; Scott and his party also reach the pole but perish on their return journey.

1914   Begins the Imperial Trans-Antarctic Expedition; the *Endurance* sails for the Weddell Sea and the *Aurora* (carrying the Ross Sea party) sails for McMurdo Sound.

1915   The *Endurance* becomes frozen in the pack ice of the Weddell Sea in late January; on November 21, the ship is crushed by the pressure of the ice pack, marooning Shackleton and his 27 men.

Shackleton and his men make an open-boat journey to Elephant Island; sails more than 800 miles to South Georgia; rescues the remaining crew on Elephant Island on August 30

Dies aboard the *Quest* off South Georgia on January 5 during fourth expedition

1914   **1917**

1916   **1922**

Begins the Imperial Trans-Antarctic Expedition; the *Endurance* sails for the Weddell Sea and the *Aurora* (carrying the Ross Sea party) for McMurdo Sound

Rescues the Ross Sea party stranded at McMurdo Sound

1916   In April, Shackleton and his men make an open-boat journey to Elephant Island; Shackleton and five other men sail more than 800 miles to South Georgia; Shackleton, Worsley, and Crean become the first men to walk across South Georgia; rescues the remaining crew on Elephant Island on August 30.

1917   Rescues the Ross Sea Party stranded at McMurdo Sound.

1921   In December, sails aboard the *Quest* on his fourth expedition, this time to circumnavigate Antarctica.

1922   Shackleton dies aboard the *Quest* off South Georgia on January 5 at age 47.

GLOSSARY

AFT   near the stern of a vessel

AMATEUR   someone without the skill of a professional

ASTERN   behind a vessel

AUXILIARY   backup or reserve

BEARING   reference of direction

CANADIAN ARCHIPELAGO   an archipelago (chain or cluster of islands) north of the Canadian mainland in the Arctic

FETLOCKS   joints in a horse's lower legs

FORE   the bow of a ship, the front

GALE   strong winds

GEOGRAPHICAL MILE   a unit to measure distance in polar exploration; equal to one minute of arc along the Equator

HEMORRHAGE   bleeding, either internally or externally

ICE FLOE   a large, thick sheet of frozen ocean water

ICE PACK   chunks and sheets of frozen ocean water tightly grouped together

INDUSTRIALIST   someone who has reached a position of prominence in a particular industry or set of industries

INTERMINABLY   seemingly without end, endlessly

INVALIDED   to release or exempt from duty because of ill health

MAROON   to abandon or isolate with little hope of ready rescue or escape

NATIONALISTIC   devotion to the interests or culture of one's nation

NATURALIST   someone educated in natural history, especially in zoology or botany

PORT   the left-hand side of a ship that is facing forward

PRESSURE RIDGE   in cases of extreme cold, ice will shrink in volume like any other solid, opening up cracks in the surface of sea water that is completely frozen over; the cracks quickly fill with water and freeze again, but when the temperature rises later, the ice expands and forces itself upward along the lines of the crack, forming jagged ridges.

PROSPECTING   exploring for mineral deposits

SASTRUGI   long, wavelike ridges of snow, formed by the wind and found on the polar plains

SCURVY   a disease caused by deficiency of vitamin C; symptoms of scurvy include spongy and bleeding gums, bleeding under the skin, and extreme weakness; if gone untreated, scurvy can be fatal.

SLEDGE   a vehicle mounted on low runners drawn by work animals, such as horses or dogs, and used for transporting loads across ice and snow

SNOW CAIRN   a mound of snow

SPAR   a wooden pole used to support sails and rigging

STARBOARD   ahe right-hand side of a ship that faces forward

SWINGLETREE   a crossbar that attaches a horse to a sledge for use in pulling

THEODOLITE   a rotating, small, mounted telescope used to measure angles in surveying, meteorology, and navigation

TILLER   a lever used to turn a rudder and steer a boat

BIBLIOGRAPHY

Alexander, Caroline. *The Endurance: Shackleton's Legendary Antarctic Expedition*. New York: Alfred A. Knopf, 1998.

Bickel, Lennard. *Shackleton's Forgotten Men: The Untold Tragedy of the Endurance Epic*. New York: Thunder's Mouth Press and Balliett & Fitzgerald, Inc., 2000.

"Ernest Shackleton." South-Pole.com. Available online at *http://www.south-pole.com/p0000097.htm*.

Heacox, Kim. *Shackleton: The Antarctic Challenge*. Washington, D.C.: National Geographic, 2008.

Huntford, Roland. *Shackleton*. New York: Atheneum, 1986.

Lansing, Alfred. *Endurance: Shackleton's Incredible Voyage*. New York: Carroll & Graf Publishers, Inc., 1999.

Morrell, Margot and Stephanie Capparell. *Shackleton's Way*. New York: Viking, 2001.

Riffenburgh, Beau. *Shackleton's Forgotten Expedition: The Voyage of the Nimrod*. New York: Bloomsbury Publishing, 2004.

"Robert Falcon Scott." South-Pole.com. Available online at *http://www.south-pole.com/p0000090.htm*.

Shackleton, Ernest. *The Heart of the Antarctic: The Farthest South Expedition, 1907–1909*. New York: Signet, 2000.

———. *South: The Story of Shackleton's Last Expedition, 1914–1917*. North Pomfret, Vt.: Trafalgar Square Publishing, 1919.

Tyler-Lewis, Kelly. *The Lost Men: The Harrowing Saga of Shackleton's Ross Sea Party*. New York: Viking, 2006.

Worsley, Frank A. *Endurance: An Epic of Polar Adventure*. New York: W.W. Norton & Company, Inc., 1999.

FURTHER RESOURCES

Huntford, Roland. *The Last Place on Earth.* New York: Modern Library, 1999.

Johnson, Nicholas. Big Dead Place: Inside the Strange and Menacing World of Antarctica. Port Townsend, Wash.: Feral House, 2005.

Thomson, David. *Scott, Shackleton, and Amundsen: Ambition and Tragedy in the Antarctic.* New York: Basic Books, 2002.

Wheeler, Sara. *Terra Incognita: Travels in Antarctica.* New York: Modern Library, 1999.

WEB SITES

Polar Explorers

http://www.polarexplorers.com

A guiding company that helps people take trips to the North or the South Pole.

Shackleton's Voyage of Endurance

http://www.pbs.org/wgbh/nova/shackleton

Information about a PBS-sponsored expedition to follow in the footsteps of Ernest Shackleton by three of the world's most distinguished mountaineers, Reinhold Messner, Conrad Anker, and Stephen Venables. Includes survival stories and interviews, photographs, and classroom resources for students and teachers.

South-Pole.com

http://www.south-pole.com/homepage.html

This site has information about the South Pole and the heroic explorers of the polar regions and the surrounding islands.

PICTURE CREDITS

INDEX

ABOUT
THE AUTHOR

LINDA DAVIS has been working with children's nonfiction books since 2006. She especially enjoys doing research for historical biographies. She lives with her family in Glencoe, Minnesota.

In Search of Teddy

Joan Greene

Published by  Hobby House Press, Inc.
Grantsville, Maryland
www.hobbyhouse.com

Additional copies of this book may be purchased at $24.95 (plus postage and handling) from
Hobby House Press, Inc.
1 Corporate Drive, Grantsville, MD 21536
1-800-554-1447
www.hobbyhouse.com
or from your favorite bookstore or dealer.
First Edition

Printed in the United States of America

ISBN: 0-87588-617-5

Acknowledgements

I always read the acknowledgements. I hope you do because you are included. Thank you to Sherry White, my editor who listened to all of my dreams for this little book and to Brenda Wiseman and Theresa Black at Hobby House. Thanks to Gary Ruddell for continuing to encourage me to write this book. Thank you to the photographers and photography assistants whom I have worked with Uldis Saule, Chuck Atkins, Jerry Cox, and Dave Marcus. Thanks to Karla Schiller, Beth Tondreau, Jerry Cox, Boram Kim, Donna Mehalko, Etta Foran, Kerry Kennedy, Dee Golfinopoulos, and Francesca Gould for editorial and creative assistance. Thank you Glenn Sousa for adding some of the best vintage photos to my collection. You all made this book possible.

To my family thank you, and to my friends who have always encouraged me to tell them my "Joan" stories: Michelle Clise, George Alexander, Susan Matthews, Kim Zuccarini, Mary Kern, Shannon Haynes, Tom and Angie Markert, Sam Rolph, Vince Roman, Carolyn Wiggins, Carolyn Cook, Howard Lunche, Greg Hay, Sharon Forrest, Elsie, Carol, and Cynthia Palmer, Trish Winstead, and Bob Stoddard.

Everyday I work with a great group of people; and although this book has been written during late evenings, weekends, and early mornings, they make my days better: Wendy Solomon, Kirk Swenk, Frank Rotundo, Boram Kim, Carrie Kellogg Garbarek, Dee Golfinopoulos, and Jim Gaddis.

This book would have never happen if it weren't for all the people who have shared their love of teddy bears with me. Thank you so much for your beautiful stories. Much gratitude to the Bears To Go Staff over the years which included store managers, Holly Evans Callan, Eve Franklin, and Lucy Tooper, and finally You. Yes, you who have taken a few moments from your hectic pace to enter the gentle world of the teddy bear. You complete the picture. I hope as you read you will feel, as I do, that we are all threads linked to one heart.

Uncle Charlie Elshire for my first teddy bear,
if you only knew what you started.

About In Search of Teddy. . .

Teddy Bears are the most pervasive, warm,
and cuddly invention of the 20th Century

The year 2002 marks the hundredth anniversary of America's most loved toy, the teddy bear. Teddy bears were popular from their beginning. By 1905, ladies could be seen bicycling through New York's Central Park with their teddies in tow and fashionable women were taking teddies to tea in Paris and London. Around 1907, Playthings Magazine reported that, although teddy bears were no longer in vogue as adult companions, they "were here to stay as children's toys."

For the next ninety years or so, teddy bears found most of their friends and relations in the nursery. The faithful ones listened to the tales of their young masters, drank tea in the backyard and often went head first down the stairs behind a short human. These teddy bears were loved into realness by soft little hands, hugged flat, and became known as excellent and patient companions for children. That is not to say that all grown-ups stopped loving teddy bears. Many a childhood bear followed its human to college or into marriage.

In Search of Teddy is the story of teddy bears and their people and the search for something often lost along the way. It is about memories sometimes clouded by distance and time. Teddy bears seem to have the ability to bring the best out in people, and in this book you will read stories about people who appreciate the beauty of a well-worn old teddy bear and the simple innocence of childhood remembered. If you are a teddy bear lover too, then like that silly ole Tigger in Pooh, you will be gazing into a looking glass and just grinning because a kindred spirit will be smiling back.

Over ninety percent of Americans
had teddy bears as childhood companions.

Contents

Introduction

Her money was tied in a soft, old cotton handkerchief that she kept at the bottom of her ancient leather handbag. I will never know her name, but her story reminds me of how fragile our lives, status, and those things that we hold most dear are. I think there is a line somewhere in the Wizard of Oz that goes something like, "My people come and go here."

By the spring of 1982, my shop, Bears To Go was beginning to get lots of local newspaper coverage, but I am getting ahead of myself. You will learn more about the adventures of a teddy bear shopkeeper as you turn the pages of this book.

It was one of those March days when the tiny leaves on the trees are that new green that you only see once a year, and a soft breeze caressed me as I crossed the parking lot to go into the store. In short, it was a day when you yearned to be in love, to be danced round and round and to be held. Spring does that to me and I think she felt the same. But she was alone, left with memories of family and friends all gone. It had taken the woman over a month just to talk someone into driving her to my shop so she could see firsthand a little Steiff that had been pictured in the newspaper article that she had saved.

She claimed that her heart stopped when she saw the bear because it was so like her childhood teddy. She pointed to the picture and asked, "Is he German?" Yes, Steiff. "Then he will understand me," her voice cracked.

Her family had fled Germany when she was very small. They only had what they could carry and in one hand she clung to her dear teddy and the other to her mother's outstretched embrace. They left everything behind, all that she knew from grandparents to the very language that she spoke. The trip to America was long and hard, but her teddy comforted her the whole way speaking softly in sweet German. When she cried herself to sleep in that new place where everything was so dark and strange, Teddy would gather her tears to him. He guarded the child and her fears. Now, once again everything that she had known was gone, her home, her family and friends. "I have out lived them all," she told me. When we met she was living in an assisted living situation. Some well-meaning relative had thought her home was too

He speaks my language

much for her to take care of, so now her life consisted of one room and her memories. And some days, she told me, her recollections of the past were all that kept her going.

I handed her the little Steiff of her dreams and hugging him close, her whole being broke out into a smile. "Oh Teddy," she kept saying over and over. And as she began to speak softly in German to the little bear, I would swear that that teddy looked right into her eyes with an understanding nod. After all, he was born German too, and it was probably like music to his little teddy bear ears to hear his native tongue being spoken.

She hands me the hankie. I untie it.

"I have been saving for him ever since I saw his picture in the paper. Three dollars should buy a nice teddy don't you think," her eyes pleaded. "Will I get change back?"

"Yes, forty-two cents." Don't ask me why forty-two cents. It was just the first amount that came to mind. I could already tell that there was very little cash in the cloth, but was equally sure that she had no idea the price of this special teddy bear. Taking the bear briefly from her gentle embrace, I removed his price tag of $78 and thanked her for the purchase.

Now, if you are an accountant or CFO or just plain can do math, you will quickly realize that I lost money on the sale of that bear. But in life, it is not really money that matters, is it? It is people and relationships, and that woman needed a friend that understood. It was my privilege to provide one for her. On the other hand, I would have given her the bear, but I remember my father telling me that whatever you do, never take away a person's pride. She needed to buy the bear and well, $2.58 was a great deal of money when all you have inside your purse is $3.07.

My own grandfather told me that he went to the movies for a nickel and could buy his date popcorn for another five cents if he had any excess cash. He claims that he rarely had two nickels so I guess he had to stand out front and miss the movie a lot. Prices and values change over the years. But what if you get to be eighty-eight or ninety or so, and you miss your childhood teddy bear and you are living on a modest income? What if you out live your family and friends? It happens. Then one day in a newspaper you see the familiar face of your childhood teddy bear that got left somewhere along the way. Who would think that a teddy bear could cost more than three dollars? Everything is relative.

Many of us cannot imagine growing
up without a teddy bear

Sometimes I wonder, will I become a bag lady? We all wonder that; don't we? Or will I get old and be alone and keep my money in a handkerchief at the bottom of my purse? If any of the above happens, I just hope I can keep one old bear that speaks my language and a human or two would be really, really nice.

Teddy bears seem to have the ability to bring the best out in people, and in this book you will read stories that mostly came to me during the twelve years that I owned a store called Bears To Go.

Many of us cannot imagine growing up without a teddy bear as our dear little friend and confidante. Teddy bears come in many sizes, shapes, and colors, so what comes to your mind's eye may be very different from everyone else. When a favorite teddy is lost or taken or given away, many a grown-up can still recall with great longing and detail their missing link to gentleness and innocence. It is not uncommon to meet an adult who, in earnest conversation, will recount the long search for their first teddy. Thus the idea for In Search of Teddy was born.

If you love teddy bears, or just the goodness that they have come to stand for, you are not alone.

"When he awoke in the morning,
the first thing he saw was
Tigger,
sitting in front of the glass
and
looking at himself.
"Hallo!" said Pooh.
"Hallo!" said Tigger.
"I've found somebody just like me.
I thought I was the only one of them."

The House at Pooh Corner

Chapter 1

Growing Up with Teddy

Teddy bears had been around a really long time when I received my first one. I recall the day like it was yesterday. My father was young and had eyes that sparkled and ears that he knew how to wiggle to make me burst into laughter. The day in question was a cool autumn Saturday and I was in the backyard when he came out to tell me that Uncle Charlie (no relation really—just an older man that my father had adopted from work) had come by to give me something very special. I was a small child, but I could tell by my father's look that no matter what the gift turned out to be I was to be polite and show gratitude.

When I entered our living room, Uncle Charlie was sitting on the end of the sofa. Propped next to him was this really big, brown craft-paper bundle. The bear inside stood silently behind the crisp paper and waited quietly like the good bear he would turn out to be. It must have been rather dark inside that package. As I unwrapped the gift, that starry-eyed, straight-armed carnival bear seemed to come alive in my imagination. He was almost my height and his big white eyes with the black dots that jiggled around looked right into my innocent, young heart. I did not have to fake my pleasure and thankfulness; it was love at first sight.

The bear who I called "Teddy" sometimes and "Blue" the rest, would see me through my childhood and become lost somehow when I left the farm to go to college. My mother claims he resides in the attic of the house that I grew up in but I have searched and searched. Teddy is gone.

The amazing thing is that, when I remember him, I can still clearly see my father and Uncle Charlie and that brown paper package. My childhood comes flooding back in memories of jeans lined in red plaid flannel, riding on my father's shoulders, vanilla salt water taffy from the State Fair, and nights spent hugging old Blue—sharing my troubles, hopes and dreams with my faithful companion.

Teddy bears can ride in wagons, fall from trees, withstand the meanest sibling and still be there when the lights go out to hold a tired little hand.

When I remember that bear,
I can still clearly see my father

And they all live on in my heart—the lost bear, the man who was my father, and a kindly older gentleman who understood that the greatest store bought present you can give a child is a teddy bear to be confidante and companion.

Maybe I was destined to be a teddy bear lady. I am not sure. Growing up, I never really played with dolls or my other toys the way that I did with Blue. I opened Bears To Go, one of the first teddy bear stores in America, on November 2, 1981. The shop attracted people like me—folks who saw something special and loving in that classic childhood companion, the teddy bear. I found that many collectors were searching, always searching, for their long-lost childhood bear. Those teddy bears that were left behind in a family move, burned after a childhood illness, who wandered away in the arms of a sibling or were mistakenly flung out of a family car window miles from home had left their mark on the hearts of many a successful adult. Now, truthfully, if Teddy were to find his way home today, his size and condition would surprise many of us. Maybe dusty memories are the real salve of our souls.

Chapter 2

The Bears Take Over My Life

Starting an all-teddy-bear-store in the early 1980s was not as difficult as landing a man on the moon, but at the time, it seemed just about as far-fetched. The main difference was that the moon trip had lots of resources behind it while I had only a dream, a job that I was afraid to quit and no money in savings.

I have vivid memories of taking my little Bears To Go business plan to conservative bankers wearing Brooks Brothers suits (them, not me) and explaining to them my business plans for a store that sold only teddy bears. The paper that the plan was printed on became almost as worn and soft as old fabric before I found one kind soul who believed in my dream. On one occasion, a seasoned older banker read the first few pages of the plan and pitched forward onto his desk. I thought he was having a heart attack right before my very eyes. I rushed around to his side of the desk to start CPR before realizing that he was doubled over with laughter.

So, from receiving a bear in a plain brown wrapper to becoming a teddy bear mogul (okay—tiny little shopkeeper) I grew up and followed the American dream of owning my own business. It did not come easily but there was a richness to the experience that I could never duplicate. Ah, what a glorious adventure. I like to think that I got a Ph. D. in business and more experience with the human spirit than my master's degree in counseling could ever give me.

To run a business on a shoestring is to aquire skills that you never dreamed you could or would want to learn. Besides meeting the people who came through those double doors, I loved creating the teddy bear mail-order catalogs. They were my way of making teddy bears come alive in pictures in much the same way that I have always believed they do on the toy store shelf as the clock strikes midnight.

My teddy bear mail order catalogs started around 1983. In those early days, I did the photography in my garden and, since it was long before the age of

*I took my
business plan
from one bank
to another*

*I finally found
one kind soul
who believed
in my dreams*

desktop publishing, I created all the catalog layouts by hand. Financing the catalog was such a hurdle that I remember once offering to sweep the printer's floor—anything to get him to publish the booklet. He wisely suggested a payment plan and that I continue to do what I did best—find homes for wayward bears.

As the catalog grew, I found a photographer listed in the yellow pages under "Passport Pictures." We taught ourselves product photography. I would arrive at the studio with a truckload of all the old props and treasures from my years of collecting. The local florist was always a stop along the way. Once I offered him the flowers from a shoot to take home to his wife. He told me that shooting the teddy bear catalog was so much more fun than what he usually did that, if he took the flowers home in such a good mood, Mrs. Marcus would be convinced he was having an affair. To this day, when I think of the photographer, Dave Marcus, my heart warms and I laugh.

The years flew by and Bears To Go eventually closed in 1993. But the things I learned and the people that I met helped forge the pathway to the life I live today. I have come a long way from the farm in Mississippi where I grew up.

Chapter 3

Chasing the American Dream

The Bears To Go Philosophy

A sign with this text hung on the walls of my little shops for over twelve years

---

About Bears To Go

The original Bears To Go opened in 1981 with the idea of offering
a gentle place to shop. The first Bears To Go opened on dreams,
a shoestring, and the belief that
each person is important.

Our goals are to offer:
A gentle place, an oasis from the hectic world
Good, knowledgeable service
The best selection of teddy bears

Teddy Bears were named after President Teddy Roosevelt and
were first made in 1902/1903. The early teddies had long arms,
were full jointed, and had a humped back.
Today, teddy bear collecting is the 4th biggest hobby in America.
Eighty percent of all worldwide teddy bear production comes to the
United States.

Bears To Go is a tale of chasing the American Dream.
We believe in what we do; and
your faces, your smiles, and your stories are an important part of
the life of this shop.
Please ask questions ~ enjoy our bears.

Joan Greene

Paul Goldammer

*To stay in business
you must have skin
like an elephant*

In the days before I opened my shop, I had little idea where to even find some of the very stock that I wanted to make the store special. One day a man came up to the grillwork that covered the entrance to the shop.

"Do you carry the German made Hermann teddy bears?" he asked.

"No, I don't carry Hermann," I answered in my usual honest manner. "I don't know where to get them . . . maybe someday."

"I can help," he said, " I sell Hermann."

And so, I made my first appointment with a sales representative.

The next day Mr. Paul Goldammer arrived at the shop's back door with three large green garbage bags full of classic German-made teddies. He simply dumped those beautiful teddy bears onto the carpet and they rolled and somersaulted over each other to get out of the plastic rubbish bags. The display was a wonderment of growling, tumbling teddy bear tradition, and they all lay at my feet waiting to be lifted up, and put on the shelves to find new homes.

I never told Mr. Goldammer, but I fondly called him "God." He had a way of showing up just when I needed him most, and he knew just when to offer encouragement and advice. It was Mr. Goldammer who told me, when my first lease was broken, that to stay in business you must have skin like an elephant. When retailing got too crazy, I remembered his wisdom and how much I learned by listening to an unassuming character that made his calls in person and delivered his wares in garbage bags. He taught me to never be too proud to ask for help, to take help when offered, to believe in miracles, that true friends trust your goodwill, and to understand that you can have a heart, but still be strong when you needed to be. Human beings tend to do things the hard way the first time around. Then, as now, valuable lessons sometimes come out of thin air and open up unseen possibilities.

A kind word or a bit of advice may be just the
serendipitous action that sets you free
to follow your heart.

Chapter 4

The Gift

I remember college art history classes. We spent hours sitting in the dark looking at slide after slide of the old masters. At the time I was bored to distraction and often took to covering page after page with doodles, drawings and weighty questions. At the ripe old age of nineteen, I had already had enough of art history. During one specific class, I started to write over and over again, "What is art? What is art?" Maybe I was just wondering what I was doing in the dark looking at Van Gogh and Renoir when I really wanted to be at the potter's wheel feeling the clay beneath my fingers. I was too young to understand the lasting value of memorizing beauty for, as my years go by, I realize that it is the memory of beauty that sustains us.

I remember so well the first Christmas I was in business. It was 1981. A young man came in looking for the right gift for his girlfriend. Something about the feeling of my shop had drawn him in, he said. I watched as his eyes landed on a soft, pure white handmade bear. Its long arms seemed to stretch out to him. His calloused hands and dirty nails were a great contrast to the snow-white bear he pulled from the shelf. I had to control every urge not to grab the bear from him. I was sure it would be returned to the shelf with black finger marks on the soft white fur. As the man turned the bear this way and that, he told me he was a car mechanic. He had worked up until the very last minute to have enough to buy one special Christmas gift.

He could have bought a gold chain or earrings, or clothing but there he was in my store reaching for one of the most expensive bears I owned. As he examined the bear, he noticed its wind-up key and began to slowly turn it. I can still see the wonder on his face when he listened to the music.

When you wish upon a star,
Makes no difference who you are. . .

His voice caught a little as he told how hard he had worked to save for his girlfriend's present and how pleased he was to find this one perfect gift.

Special is something that you feel

I have often wondered what made him reach for that bear when reason would have said that a young guy like him would go for something more regular, more practical—flashier. But the automobile mechanic had the soul of an artist. He knew art when he saw it and carefully counted out the cash to make that one Christmas purchase.

Did the recipient of that gift have any idea what an extraordinary person she knew? He understood quality over quantity. He understood that "special" is something you feel. It is not about the name on the box or the newest trend. It is about an object that tugs at your heart and imprints on your being with a kind of gentle sigh.

I wish I could tell you the end of the story. Where is the man today? Is he still an artist at living life? Has time changed his gentle spirit? And the girl, does she still have that snow-white bear? Does he still play "When You Wish Upon a Star?"

The movies of my mind play the scene over and over from that long-closed teddy bear shop. I see the young mechanic's stained hands, the white bear, and the gift-wrapped package he carried without a bag so as not to crush the bow.

I marvel that nineteen years later one act of kindness remains archived in my heart as if I was the one who received that wonderful present. And I was, I guess. The man was one of the greatest gifts of my twelve years in business. You see, people are more than appearances. And the gentlest heart might come with work-worn hands.

Chapter 5

Tattered Teddies and Their Tales

Within the first month of opening my teddy bear shop, I got into something I never expected. It was early one morning. I had not even turned on the lights, opened the register, or given the bears their wake up fluff when I noticed two frail, properly dressed elderly ladies standing by the front door of the shop. Do you remember blue-tinted gray hair? They both had the exact same shade of gray/blue hair and wore closely matching Channel suits of contrasting colors. I will never be sure how long the women had waited outside the door—five minutes or five hours. Their sad, patient faces told me instantly that they were not there to purchase a bear, or a birthday card, or such. They were on a mission. One was holding onto the other's elbow, and in her other arm she cradled a bundle wrapped in a soft, pale bath towel. They looked scared and, for a moment, I thought they were two little old angels about to leave a tiny child by the door of Bears To Go. Instead, as soon as I could get the door opened the "take-charge" sister moved swiftly to my counter and placed her bundle on top.

"My sister was up all night," she said, "so we dressed at dawn and I braved the freeway to get here."

I wish you could have seen them. Now, if I had been up all night dealing with an emergency, I would have pulled on a pair of old jeans and a sweatshirt to go for help. Not those two. They were dressed to the nines, complete with hose, suits, jewelry and those little handbags that fasten shut with a gold clasp in the center.

It seems that Teddy had fallen out of bed the night before and broken his neck. As the woman unfolded the towel, I realized that inside was a sixteen to eighteen-inch early Steiff bear whose head was no longer joined to his body. Teddy had slept with the now very sad sister since she was a baby—night after night for over seventy years—but the precious bear had become careless and fallen to the hard floor below. Brittle joints are almost as

She was lost without him

common in old bears as they are in older humans. Teddy had lost all of his dignity and was in need of emergency care. Why, there he sat in front of a total stranger, head in his hands. His serious condition had rendered his owner sleepless and worried. It was far too late in life to be left without her dear little bear. "She is lost without him," she said, "he has been with her all her life—they are twins, you know, Teddy and my sister."

I recall wondering what on earth to do. I knew zero, nada, nothing about teddy bear repair and it was the Christmas holiday season, my make-or-break-it time at the shop. I did not even have a needle and thread in the store. But I had a dear lady standing in front of me who would not sleep until Teddy was whole again. So I did what any caring human being would do. I closed the shop, called a bear-maker friend and began my first teddy bear surgery.

By four o'clock I was back in business at the store. Teddy sat sporting a new bow as he waited for the sisters to reclaim him. Oh, his head was still a little saggy. He had not slept a wink the night before, you know, and he had undergone major surgery that very day.

After they retrieved him, I never saw the sisters or Teddy again. They drove north to Daly City or San Bruno, California, or somewhere miles away from my store. I can still see the smile on the owner's face as she reached for Teddy and gave him a little hug. Although she wasn't one for public shows of affection, I am sure, she could not help herself when Teddy held up his head to let her know that all was well. The sister who drove stepped forward to take my hand and thank me. And off they went, two blue/gray-haired ladies and one happy old Steiff with a new red ribbon that he could hardly wait to exchange for a soft nightshirt.

Chapter 6

Teddy, Come Home

I opened Bears To Go to sell new teddy bears, but the truth was that old bears sometimes lose an eye, or fall out of bed and lose their head, or an ear comes loose from being tugged along by a child. Whatever the reason, old teddy bears need repairs from time to time. That which started as an act of kindness for two elderly sisters turned into my becoming somewhat of a specialist in teddy bear surgery. Some repairs were simply easier than others, and in some cases the doctor fell in love with the patient, and that made the relationship very complex.

Did you ever fall desperately in love with something that would never be yours, could never belong to you, and in fact, already belonged to someone else? Such was the case of another teddy bear that came to me for repairs. I will never forget the first time I laid eyes on that large old grayed Steiff bear. I cannot think of any toy, work of art—or anything for that matter—that has ever pulled at my heart so much on initial glance. It was love at first sight.

It was just before Christmas 1982 and the old teddy bear and his lifelong companion, Bully, an antique Steiff bulldog, were brought to me for repairs. Teddy and Bully had belonged to a Mrs. Smith of San Francisco for many years. The bear and the dog had outlived many of her best friends and beloved relatives, but she had begun to worry about Teddy's drooping head and Bully's growing worn spots.

That Christmas season her niece brought them to me for repairs with instructions to finish them before Christmas Eve. Whatever day of the week it was—Thursday, I think—the love affair began, for in my hands was the most perfect teddy bear I had ever seen. I know that, if that old bear could have talked, he would have shared universal truths and the keys to the mysteries of life. His look held me and, to this day, I can see his face.

As in a human love affair, I mostly spent time gazing at the bear. For weeks he sat un-repaired on my sofa. I would bring home little gifts for him—

On the last day we had together
we sat for our portrait.
He lives in my heart—the tilt of his head,
the wise old eyes . . .

a pair of wire-rimmed glasses, a big silk bow and an old book to keep him busy while I was away. Still I could not find the strength inside myself to open his seams and begin the repairs. To me, Teddy was perfect. His drooping head was just a sign of age like his graying hair. I could tell by the areas around his joints that he had once been a warm cinnamon color but over the years he had turned a beautiful silvery gray.

As Christmas Eve drew closer, I thought of his real owner and how sad her holiday would be without her longtime friend, so I set aside a day to repair my beloved. As I opened him, I got the feeling that his original maker at the Steiff factory had felt the power of this guy, too. The maker who had birthed Teddy had left a secret inside the bear. It was as if she had wanted to freeze time inside that bear so she had carefully tucked a folded newspaper and her bear maker's tool, a needle, inside his chest. The needle and newspaper seemed to be carefully placed as they were encased in a square of folded fabric.

I have seen amazing things stuffed inside of German-made bears, everything from clothing to wadded newspaper, but this did not seem to be part of a careless act or a lack of excelsior that day. It was as if the person who sewed up the new bear said, "Here Teddy, good luck, take a part of me with you."

For all those years, years before my birth or even the birth of my mother, the old bear had carried the secret of his maker near his heart. As I sewed him up I added a new secret. Tucked in with the old needle and paper was a brand-new note that read, "Teddy Come Home," with my name and address.

On his last day with me, I had our portrait made together and for years I have waited. Never before or since have I left a message inside a teddy bear that I repaired. I am writing this around the holidays, and this year I think maybe, just maybe that old teddy bear will find his way into my arms. It doesn't really matter. Oh, I would love to see him under the tree this year, but no matter, he lives in my heart—the tilt of his head, the wise old eyes. I wonder, how could one old toy mean so much to this modern woman?

When the repairs were complete, the old guy, with lifted head, looked into my soul and smiled. I am a dreamer—age and life have left me that—and to this day I believe that someday he will come home to me.

And if I had the house by the sea,
I would take up the quest
to possess him once again.

So he could gaze peacefully out
across the water.

I often think of the old gray Steiff and believe that, if there was one object in this world that I could request and find on my doorstep, I would ask for that bear. His understanding eyes that pierced my soul are branded on my mind. I can see him with instant recall. I can think of only one thing that I might trade him for if he were mine—a house by the sea. And, if I had the house by the sea, I would take up the quest to possess him once again so he could sit in a window box and gaze peacefully out across the water.

I have often told the story of Gray Bear, how much I love him and the note tucked inside his chest begging him to come home to me. In the late 1990s, I received a letter from Bette Carter, a former police officer turned teddy bear maker who told me that my story inspired her to create a teddy bear named Paddy. Paddy comes with a compass tied around his neck and a note that reads, "If far away from you I should roam, with this compass I'll find my way back home." If only we all came equipped with a compass to help us find our way back to all those people and things that we have left along the path of our lives.

By the way, if you are ever repairing an old gray Steiff bear with liquid black eyes and find my name inside, will you please send him home to me? I have been waiting a long time now.

I have often told the story of how much I love him.

Chapter 7

Mysterious Ways

God works in mysterious ways.

It was another busy Christmas for Bears To Go. I don't recall the exact year, but I think it was the year of Teddy Ruxpin and another talking teddy called AG Bear. The Wall Street Journal had mentioned Bears To Go. Reporter Charles Osgood had interviewed me in the store for an opening piece on CBS News with Dan Rather. Teddy bears were hot and the people came in droves for our bears. Hardly a teddy went without a home that year.

Of course, with great prosperity comes certain problems—oops—let's say "challenges." The store itself was barely eight hundred square feet in size and, in anticipation of Christmas, every flat surface was covered with teddy bears. There was hardly enough room to walk through the shop the Saturday before Christmas. Those were the days before cash register scanners and we were rather old-fashioned in comparison to other merchants anyway.

By mid-morning on the Saturday in question, there was a line of people probably twenty or thirty deep, that wove its way around the store. Each customer got our full attention once at the register. But getting there was another story. Our happy Christmas tape was playing, a couple of babies were crying, a tree filled with teddy bear ornaments threatened to capsize and the natives were starting to get restless, asserting that someone with a stroller had broken into the line.

Suddenly a tall, red-haired man with freckles and a bright plaid shirt stepped out of his place in the line. In one quick move he grabbed three innocent teddy bears and began to juggle them—really juggle them—moving from one end of the line to the other. Soon people started to laugh and talk with each other and forget that they had a ton of errands to do before the day was over. At that very minute, they wanted to be in that bear store. Everything had changed with that one kind act. Being in line was not so bad. Harried Christmas shoppers actually gave way to enjoying the moment as the entertainment was so outstanding.

In anticipation of
Christmas,
every flat surface
was covered with
teddy bears.

When the line was finally almost down to the last person, the juggler stepped forward to make his own purchases. Was he a professional juggler or clown or performer, I asked?

"Well, sort of," he said, as he leaned over the counter.

"Well, what does sort of mean?" I asked.

"Minister," he answered, as he took the bag and waved goodbye. It turns out that God does work in mysterious ways. And that, folks, was the juggler's finest hour—a real sermon without notes or choir or pews.

That teddy bear store was a constant source of amazing days and unique memories. There was the sit-in when a group of local Berkeley women noticed the polar bear cub in my window and decided that it was a real, stuffed polar bear. Now, this was no ordinary plush polar, but an amazingly realistic looking Artic cub. Standing on his hind legs, the bear stands almost five feet tall. Everything about him looks real from his lifelike glass eyes, to his long hand-carved claws. This guy could easily be a stand in for a movie. You know, one of those scenes where the glacier is too cold or dangerous for the live star and they send in the stunt guy or in this case the stuffed one.

One morning I rounded the bend to my store to find a group of townsfolk blocking the door. You know what they say about word of mouth. One person had told another person and so on until a crowd gathered to protest the unthinkable—a teddy bear store displaying a stuffed, dead bear. It took my local friendly policemen to get the angry mob to move just enough so I could squeeze into the shop.

Berkeley the Bear
Currently Retired
Former Display Window Star

Even after I took the offending bear out of the window and brought him out front to show them that he was, in fact, a hand-made acrylic plush bear there were doubters. How could anyone make a bear that looked so lifelike? What an introduction to the city of Berkeley that poor frightened bear had.

As the years went by he became the star of every window and a celebrity in town for his realistic appearance. Several from the mob claimed that they were the first to realize that he was just a really good fake. He became so tied to the lore of that area of Berkeley that he actually took on the name, Berkeley or the one he likes better, Berk for short. That bear's starring roles varied from a stint dressed as one of Roosevelt's Rough Riders, a few weeks as a large disgruntled Easter Bunny Bear (try getting a tiny colored egg from a polar bear), to tall guy lifting another teddy up to place the star on top of the Christmas Tree. Sometimes he would go on location to the other Bears To Go at Ghirardelli Square in San Francisco where he worked as a gardener, chef, ghost, and in parts large and small too numerous to mention here. The amusing thing was when he was off on loan to the city shop, folks would stop by and ask what happened to Berk. It was an unwritten rule that that bear could never be sold. He belonged to us all, his adoring public.

Today Berkeley has retired from public life and can be seen looking out my living room window. Through winter and summer, he has a wonderful view of Chicago's skyline. He has taken on the persona of a retired senator and has traded in all the costumes he wore over the years for his favorite— a regal red, white, and blue Masonic sash trimmed in real gold fringe.

Chapter 8

Dreams, Shoestrings, and a Cult

To keep with the theme of God working in mysterious ways, I want to tell you about one of the most extraordinary days of my life. It was a bleak Friday afternoon in 1985. We were down to the wire that month. The rent was due, the teddy bear suppliers' bills needed to be paid and the light bill was staring me in the face. Our sales were just off. That was all there was to it. Nothing was working. Our customers were going to the beach or buying clothes or housewares or back-to-school gear—something—but they were not buying teddy bears, as far as I could tell.

Now, America's small businesses often run on dreams and a shoestring. I would have put on a sandwich board and walked the streets of Berkeley if I thought it would have made a difference. But my sense was that we were just not going to make it through the month. Still, every day in the retail world is a new day, full of fresh hope. But as the hours ticked by, hope was dying. I remember saying to Heather, who worked for me, that I thought I would just go home and shoot myself. The truth is that the only gun I own shoots water and does not deliver much of a blow, but children and clowns love it. I was just being dramatic and had no intentions of the sort, but I did eventually leave the miserable situation to Heather's capable hands.

As I headed home, I said a little prayer to God to save the bear store. Where, I reasoned, would all those homeless bears go if they no longer had the shelter of Bears To Go? Then I felt guilty for asking God for such a frivolous request and apologized to Him the rest of the way home.

Now, remember, as I walked out the door of the teddy bear store I had told poor Heather that I was headed home to shoot myself. Arriving at my apartment, I noticed a tiny moving fluff ball hanging out of my sixth floor apartment window. My heart stopped. Was that my sweet cat, Groucho?

I parked the car, in the middle of the street, I think, and raced into the building and up to my apartment. I ran to the bathroom window where the cat's meow had become very weak as she hung on by her claws to the side of the brick building. How long had she been there? How was I going to get her down? I opened the window wide and, after climbing up on the toilet, leaned out the window. I leaned further and further until my hands could feel my grouchy cat. I had her, thank God!

Then my feet slipped, the window banged shut and there we were—scared cat and worried shopkeeper—hanging on the side of a six-story building. As the blood ran to my head, all I could think about were my last words to Heather. Now, quite by accident, I was going head first out my window. I could just imagine the report in the daily papers: "Distraught teddy bear storeowner jumps to her death, taking her innocent cat with her." The guy from Channel Something News would stand outside the art deco entrance of my building, microphone in hand, and my neighbors would recount that they had heard that teddy bear sales were off that summer.

Okay, back to the scene of the crime. Thank goodness. My feet caught and somehow, I will never know how—I was younger and fitter then—I pulled the cat and myself back into the bathroom. I sat on the floor for what seemed like forever just shaking and thanking God with the cat licking my face. We were both wrecks.

A ringing telephone brought me out of my crazed stupor. It was Heather.

"We are alive over here, Heather," I kept assuring her.

I am sure she thought I had lost my mind, but her next words brought me instantly back to reality.

"Come get the rent money," she said.

I looked at the clock on my bedside table. Three hours had passed since I left. Had Heather been so worried about the store that she robbed a bank?

"Hold on," I told her.

My wobbly legs took me down to the car and off I went back to Berkeley. When I arrived at the store, Heather's eyes were all sparkly and she was laughing like a fool, out of control—crazed. What was happening? Was this all a dream?

It turns out someone was listening when I prayed for help and had ignored my apologies. About thirty minutes after I had left—about the time I was hanging on the side of the building—a bus had pulled up in front of Bears To Go. A man in a conservative business suit, carrying a walkie-talkie approached Heather and asked if he could check the store—stock room and all—for safety. He had clients who wanted to come shopping there but he had to make sure that the coast was clear. (Are you beginning to think this is a plot for a sitcom?) I swear it is all true. I just know someday when I am old and tell this story they will put me in the loony bin.

Well, the man motioned for the occupants of the bus to come in and an entire cult, all dressed in flowing robes and with cult-like names, came shopping in that miserable little bear store that afternoon. And buy, they did with cold, hard cash, no less. By the time I got there, Heather had a little over three thousand dollars in a bag.

The next day they came back—or at least one of them did and spent another $1,200. And the bears were saved, the rent got paid on time and the store went on to open a second location in Ghirardelli Square at Fisherman's Wharf in San Francisco.

For the next seven years, we continued to find homes for the teddy bears that graced our shelves. And, no, the cult never came back again. Was it all a dream? All I know is that the cash was real and the cat lived to be at least 16 or 18 years old. And, thank heavens, the cult—whoever they were—decided to take a field trip that day. I wonder if the bears they bought are chanting and eating seaweed and whole grains? Or did the cult break up—each member taking a bear to Wall Street or Laguna Beach? I will never know. But I tell you there was a day in the late summer of 1985 when I was about to give up, my cat almost committed suicide and a cult really did come shopping, and they saved—really saved—Bears To Go.

For years we continued to find homes for the teddy bears that graced our shelves

Chapter 9

Hobos, Bag Ladies and a Balloon Man

In the years I had a shop at the top of the steps at Ghirardelli Square, I had customers from the most famous movie stars to a bag lady named Sara Jane. And it is Sara Jane I want to tell you about.

For years I had seen her walking the streets of San Francisco's fashionable Union Square and the North Beach area. Her shoulders were always rounded forward from the weight of her two full shopping bags. Hers was a familiar face but who she was never really occurred to me until I looked up one day to find her in my store.

The tourists and other customers left immediately as she carried a perfume of dust, human smells and old wool. How could they be expected to shop with a bag lady? She straightened up as she set her burdens down on my beautifully carpeted floor.

"I want a bear," she announced loudly.

Of course I thought that meant for free and I wondered which little bear would fit in her overstuffed bags.

"I can pay and I know exactly which bear I want," she said. "That big one in the window—and I want a nice, green bow around it's neck. The pink one won't match my living room. How much?"

Her hand disappeared into the neck of her dress, all the way deep inside of her bra, and she brought out a wad of bills. As she counted out the money, she told me her name was Sara Jane.

"Remember that name," she almost begged me. "I'm going to be your best customer. I pay in cash, you know," she added laughing, "And, by the way, would you box up that bear? I will pick him up tomorrow—and remember the green ribbon. 'Night, Joan, nice meeting you. It's been a long time since someone shook my hand," she sighed. "I'm going to be your best customer." After she left, I took the bear out of the window and put the big green bow around his neck. I just stood there wondering. Did the bag lady really have a living room? Would she be back? The next day she was back. First, she quizzed me to see if I remembered her name.

She was
probably a sassy

little girl

"Sure. How are you Sara?"

"No, no. The name is Sara Jane," she insisted. "A name is everything. Promise you will remember my name." And I did.

She bought one or two more teddy bears, but whenever she was in my neighborhood, she would stop by to say hello and to make sure that I knew her name.

For years my friends did not know whether to be amazed or embarrassed when we were walking down a street in San Francisco and a clear old voice would yell out to me, "Hi, Joan!" And I would yell back, "Hi, Sara Jane!" I always stopped to introduce her and to tell whomever I was with that she was my best customer. She would never take a nickel from me. "We are friends," she would say.

In Berkeley we had our balloon man. He was a mentally challenged man who walked the streets of Berkeley. He was tall and so thin. His clothes were always disheveled and somewhat soiled. He definitely was not the guy you wanted hanging out at a genteel teddy bear store. So, of course, what was his favorite shop in all of Berkeley? Bears To Go, where else?

Every day, for all the years that we were in Berkeley, he stopped by at least once a day, sometimes twice. He would buy a helium balloon and ask me to tie the end of the ribbon to a dirty, old styrofoam coffee cup. And I did. Then he would walk outside the door, look up in the sky as if it was the way out, and let go of the balloon.

I never understood the appeal of that flight but, come ran or shine, he was there. I am sure he ran some customers off—the crazy-looking guy with the balloon just walking around drooling on the bears. Now, I should have wanted to move him down the road. But I didn't. He was just part of the landscape at Bears To Go. Love my store, love my balloon man, you might say.

Come to think of it, he was in the store that Christmas morning when the minister started to juggle the bears. It must have looked like a circus—the tall, red-haired juggler, the grungy balloon man, John Denver and the Muppets singing over the speakers, and the Christmas rush. Still the teddy bear lovers came. Why, I am not sure, but I think it had something to do with being real.

From day to day, a shop takes on its own life and there are "regulars" who come back over and over to buy or just visit. Then again, almost daily even after you have been in business for years, someone finds you for the first time. If you look for the wonder everyday, it comes in the customer who stops to tell you about a new grandchild or to share their grief. The days pass quickly by until you wake up one morning and realize that you have been there for years. And you love your great customers or guests, as they are called these days, but you get your spice from the people like Sara Jane, or the Balloon Man, or the Hobo that I am about to tell you about.

The display windows at my tiny shop in San Francisco's Ghirardelli Square were well loved throughout the city. I spent many a late night or early morning creating scenes for the teddy bears to star in. The bears did everything in the windows, from laundry to barbecuing stuffed fish on a Weber grill. In the wee hours of the morning, changing the windows often seemed like a thankless task. But, later in the day, I would see a child pull at her parent's hand to stop for a look. Or I'd hear a passerby laugh out loud at the folly of those window bears.

One particular night stands out in my memory. It was around 2 a.m. I was just finishing a new window when I saw what appeared to be a honeymooning couple stop to steal a kiss. The bears were gardening—with real dirt on the floor of the display and real flowers springing up from the rich, moss-covered earth. Just as the couple was about to walk away, a ragged, weathered hobo stepped out of the shadows of the building to tell them that, when he was a little down, he always made the trek to Ghirardelli Square to see the teddy bear store windows. "They have more heart than any window in the town," I heard him say. Suddenly, all the work it took to make each window unique and special seemed worthwhile.

I remember thinking that he could probably use a hot meal. That was the least I could do for the warmth his comments had given me. So I took a twenty-dollar bill from my purse, locked the shop and went in search of the man. I did not have far to go. He was sitting on a bench near the fountain upstairs. So I walked up to him, introduced myself and thanked him for

noticing my windows. I extended my hand, with the money in it, and told him I hoped it would buy him something he needed. Suddenly the twinkle of a much younger man gleamed in his eyes and he took my hand and asked me if I would like to go dancing. It seems it had been a really long time since he had seen so much money and all he could think of was dancing. I have always been too serious, I guess. I did not go dancing with the hobo of a man. It was missed opportunity as I never saw him again.

No matter, until the day we closed our doors, those windows were filled with magic and the dreams of the child that lives in all our hearts. Once there was a gorilla and a big brown bear who played poker while drinking "Bear Beer." The gorilla held a winning card behind his back, supplied by a big, plush basset hound. That group caused such a stir that a customer actually sent her limousine driver to fetch the entire scene—gorilla, trick dog and good loser bear. I think I saw the gorilla wave good-bye as the chauffeur carried him down those long front steps at Ghirardelli Square.

Every day for a month before we closed in Berkeley, I walked the Balloon Man to a new store that I had gotten to agree to sell him balloons for his quarter a day. In the years that passed by, I designed teddy bears for several large companies including Hallmark Cards, Inc., and I moved from the San Francisco Bay Area never again to see Sara Jane (remember that name).

With childlike innocence, the vibrato of youth, and an artist's heart, I was able to chase the American Dream and win. Open for business meant being open to all the joy and wonder that the unique human beings of this world brought with them as they crossed the threshold into the world that I created. And none of us can ever be the same, because we once touched each other – the Teddy Bear Lady, the thousands of guests, the Bag Lady, the Balloon Man, and the Hobo.

Chapter 10

For the Love of Bears

Because the bear store was my home for over twelve years, friends got a kick out of thinking of ways to help out. One just showed up one hot Saturday in a full plush teddy bear suit he had rented. That must have been the slow summer of 1985.

Then there was the book signing for a book about gummi bears going to camp. There just wasn't a following for such a book, although there are many gummi bear lovers. So I called in friends who brought friends to buy a book that told about how to tell the sex of a gummi bear by the color of the jelly creation.

Every Bears To Go event seemed to have the air of a three-ring circus. There were always people who just saw the notice and showed up with their wares. I didn't have the heart to turn them away. After all, this is America, the land of free enterprise. There would be people selling teddy bears on the sidewalk outside my store while I was trying to make ends meet inside the shop I was renting. Book authors would show up with stacks of books and a card table.

Then there were the school field trips. The bear store was a magnet for kindergarten and grade school field trips. Many a morning I would look up and there would be thirty little teddy bear lovers hanging onto a rope they all shared to help them stay together. There is something about a child and a bear. They seem to recognize each other immediately.

Once a stray child wandered in and, frankly, I was worried enough to call security to help me find her parents. A shop in a tourist area can get pretty busy on a summer's day and I was afraid that this little one might be lost. She seemed happy enough hugging bears. She even informed me that she had never had a teddy bear. Of course, I could remedy that situation. So I told her to pick a bear that she liked and we waited to see to whom she belonged.

Suddenly, a frantic teacher and a bus load of children descended on Bears To Go. The happy child showed her new bear all around. Then the teacher chastised me for giving one child a bear and disappointing all the other children. Now, that is no way to talk to a teddy bear lady. So I opened the stock room and gave out thirty something matching bears to the other children and the teacher. Never heard another word. Maybe the word had gotten around and I was the victim of a kindergarten con.

For years I wrote a free teddy bear newsletter that went out to bear lovers around the San Francisco Bay Area. One day I got a call from a man who lived in an apartment complex in Foster City just south of San Francisco. It seems that for years he would watch for the teddy bear newsletter that was being sent to someone else in the building. He'd snag the thing and read it. For some reason he was feeling guilty about stealing teddy bear newsletters and called to admit his sin and ask for a copy of his own. I am not sure he was a teddy bear collector but he was certainly a collector of teddy bear stories.

I hated to close the store for people like the newsletter thief, the balloon man, the bag lady, and the child in each person who walked through the door and fell in love with a teddy bear. The shops were made of dreams of the child that had grown up on a farm in Mississippi with a bear named Blue. I would go to Paris and Africa, and marry a prince. So the walls of the store were covered with hand silkscreened wallpaper sent all the way from Paris, and some of the bears did make it to Africa. For a number of years I was able to create a special place that offered gentleness to people hungry for kindness and a respite from this hurried world.

Wherever I go, whatever I do,
deep in my heart lives a teddy bear lady
frozen in time.

Chapter 11

Men and Their Bears

Nearly everybody, given the right impetus, has a teddy bear story to share. For example, an aging business executive at a party tells about living overseas for a year as a child. Because they needed to travel light, the family was very restricted in the number of children's toys that they could bring. There were three children in the family and only one teddy bear. So each night his mother would give the bear to the youngest to go to sleep with, then moved the bear onto the middle one until he went to sleep and finally to the oldest child who got to keep the bear the rest of the night.

Research has shown that most Americans owned teddy bears when they were children. Few, it would seem, ever put those bears completely out of their hearts. Today, as has been true for a century, children still enjoy teddy bears as companions. Although stuffed dogs, pigs, cats, monkeys and others have their moments of glory, it is the teddy bear that goes on forever.

In the days that I had my shop (1981-1992) there was even a San Francisco newsman who often recounted his tales of a bear that he was rather fond of. Bill's bear was a soft plop of a guy called Snuffles made by the American toy company, Gund. San Francisco Examiner columnist, Bill Mandel, claimed he never had a teddy bear until he was in his 30s and the bear came to him by way of a girlfriend. When the woman left, Bill found himself hugging the bear at night and not wanting to give it up.

The basic truth for Bill was that all parts of the day go better with bears. Naturally, they improve one's sleep immeasurably. Bears are better than a drink when you get home after a hard day. They'll listen to all the complaints your human companions just pretend to hear. They are discreet to a fault. If you must have a stiff drink anyway, bears will not criticize you, and they are economical, too—they're teetotalers. Finally, bears allow adults to play like kids and that is one of the secrets to their success.

I once read about an insurance adjuster who went to settle the claims on a disastrous fire in the Reno, Nevada area. On his last day there, he saw a big teddy bear in his hotel gift shop that seemed perfect for his grandchild. Because it was too big for a bag, the man walked through the hotel carrying

The bear was a soft plop of a guy

the large bear. Deciding to have a cocktail, he sat down in the bar and tossed the bear into the chair next to him. The barmaid refused to serve him for rough treatment of a bear, but the keno attendant did sell the bear a ticket. The man finally got a drink when the bear won $12,500 on the ticket.

See, teddy bears really are good luck.

The stories of men and their teddy bears are as varied as the people and circumstances that they found themselves in. From confidants, to good luck charms, to offering supreme comfort there seems to be a spot in most people's heart for a teddy bear.

I am never sure how to tell the teddy bear story that's closest to my heart without making others feel sad. Like so many of the stories of my life, it's inextricably linked with a teddy bear.

There is something about
unconditional love,
dogs,

little boys,

and
teddy bears

When my husband, Dave and I first met, I gave him a little bear he called BB (for Briefcase Bear). BB went everywhere that Dave went. He even took his vacation with us and acquired his own surfing gear. At one point while walking through a teddy bear show with Dave, BB fell helplessly, hopelessly in love with Helga, a vintage Troll doll. The two became a couple and Dave and I enjoyed making up stories about the life that BB and Helga shared.

On the day that Dave died, he struggled so and did not want to go. He didn't want to leave me alone. Hours and hours passed and he was in so much pain that I could hardly stand it anymore. Suddenly I thought of BB. I let go of Dave's hand, ran into his study and grabbed BB. When I came back into the room, I put BB into Dave's hand and closed his fingers around the little bear. I told him that I loved him, but that he had to go and that BB had always gone with him when I couldn't, so BB was there to help him. Within minutes, Dave's face relaxed a bit as he grasped BB. In the end, that little bear of his helped him through to a journey that only Dave could take.

Today BB and Helga live on the dresser next to my bed. Helga still looks young and a bit silly with her yellow Troll hair braided in pigtails, but BB has this wise, kind look about his eyes as if he has completed the mission he came for. And so he did. At barely four inches tall, that tiny Steiff teddy amused, amazed and comforted his six-foot, all-grown-up human. What more could you ask from a teddy bear?

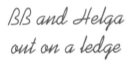

BB and Helga out on a ledge

Chapter 12

My Teddy Bears

You know you are a true collector when you spend your house payment on an old teddy bear. And that is how another BB Bear came to live with me.

First, I should explain that, in this case, BB stands for basketball-head bear, not to be confused with BB, the briefcase bear or any other BB that you might know. Please don't tell him. It would hurt his feelings. But from the moment I saw him across a crowded antique show, BB's head appeared to me to be patterned after a basketball with teddy bear ears attached. It is his soul that attracted me to him.

One Sunday morning a number of years ago, I decided to stop by a local antique show to browse for an hour or two before I had to open my shop. Within no time I had spotted the most wonderful teddy bear. He was just too expensive for my budget, so I patted him on the head and walked away.

Have you ever seen something—an inanimate object—that just took your breath away and touched you deep inside? Just looking at that bear made me want to cry and hold him to me. But I walked away determined to live without him and his high price tag.

An hour passed and I knew I needed to at least think about leaving. I realized that I really had not seen another thing after spotting BB. I kept rounding the booth and glancing at him. Each time I would get near him my heart would almost stop as the thought crossed my mind that maybe he was gone. He was such a fine teddy bear.

Then it happened. On my umpteenth trip by him, I felt like my feet were made of lead and I could not get enough air. He was missing. I rushed up to the antique dealer.

"What happened to the old bear that was here a few minutes ago?" I cried.

Isn't it funny how when something is gone,
we suddenly realize its value?

"I think he is sold," she said. "A customer is taking him over to her husband to look at."

Isn't it funny how when something is gone, we suddenly realize its value? I could see him looking over the lady's shoulder and one paw was in the air as if waving good-bye or HELP ME.

When the lady returned to try to get a better deal on the bear she made two fatal mistakes. First, she set the bear down. Secondly, she told the retailer that he was a worn old bear and that she wanted a better price. The bear looked at me as if begging me to get him out of there. Before you could say teddy bear five times, I whipped out my checkbook, paid full price for the worn old bear and hurried out of the building. It is a miracle that the bear and I are not living on the street because, in my altered state, I had just spent my entire house payment on a teddy bear.

Now, I have never regretted for one moment the day that I bailed BB out of the clutches of a collector who did not understand his value. He is a big bear, standing almost three feet tall, and over the years, I have indulged him with a full wardrobe from a Victorian sailor suit to a vintage baseball uniform. Every bear in my collection loves him, and my only antique porcelain doll has adopted him as her own. I have photographed him in every pose and with every prop that I can find. I always tell anyone who stays at my house that, in case of emergency, there are two things that they must try to save—my real, live dog, Dottie, and my beautiful BB bear. When I look at that bear's face I remember my old blue bear, my father, my uncle Charlie and my childhood, all of which are now only memories reflected back through the eyes of a kind old bear.

Chapter 13

Growing Up with Teddy

Viola Russ McBride was born at the end of the Victorian Era. She grew up to save the town of Ferndale, California, from the "modernization" that occurred across many of America's rural towns in the 1960s. Rather than see the wooden gingerbread building facades changed to brick and aluminum siding, Viola purchased most of her sleepy little Victorian town.

When I met Mrs. McBride, she was pretty much in retirement and I was told she hardly ever gave an interview anymore. She was tired of explaining why she had saved the town, but when I told her that I owned a teddy bear store, she offered to meet me in her office. After she decided she liked me, she took me to her beautiful house.

Her home, like her life, was filled with treasures dating all the way back to the turn of the twentieth century. When asked what she most cherished, she noted her relationships and something upstairs that she rarely showed a stranger. As we journeyed up the stairs, I could only guess what waited there. Before long I was shown a carefully folded and refolded article about a sixth birthday party and the pink butterfly wings that were given to the little guests at the Russ home. Then I was introduced to two little well-loved teddy bears.

"They raised me you know," Viola said.

Viola's grandfather, Joseph Russ, was one of the earliest settlers in this lush, redwood-forested area on the far northern coast of California. Viola actually remembered being hidden under her grandmother's big skirt for an entire day during an Indian raid. She had grown up in a time of soft white lace, candlelight and violet-scented toilette water in an area of the country that was anything but gentle. There off the coast of California was the juxtaposition of refined New England pioneer families, the wild sea, the rugged coast and the American Indians who roamed the forest they had long called their own.

Viola Russ McBride

Those were the days before electric lights and it was an alert teddy that could hear the cries in the dark of a motherless child

Viola was one of the first American cowgirls, actually managing her family's estate and riding the range to herd cattle. And this pioneer and visionary businesswoman told me a touching tale of being raised by two little twin teddy bears.

Viola remembered her mother in misty swatches like seeing someone's image in the ripples of a bright clear lake. You can see it and yet you can't, so one is forced to look up to see the real person. In Viola's case, her mother died soon after her sixth birthday and only one special gift can bring back a clear vision of her dear young mother. Viola does remember how much her mother loved her and the wonderful sixth birthday party her mother gave her.

Viola still has her mother's gift from that fateful day. As she floated on gossamer butterfly wings she had no idea she would soon be left without her mother and be moved from the city to the wild northwest to grow up with her grandmother and aunts. What could a dying mother leave a sweet, innocent only child that would protect and give her comfort?

Mrs. Russ gave Viola two perfectly matched white Steiff teddy bears. She reasoned that, if one wore out, Viola would have a second one to help her through childhood. Viola says they were kept in the bottom drawer of her dresser and she would take out one at a time to be her companion and sleeping mate. Those were the days before electric lights and telephones and once the candle was blown out, it was an alert teddy that could hear the cries in the dark of a motherless child.

When I met Viola, she had lived through everything from two world wars to the fall of the Berlin Wall. She was a businesswoman, cowgirl, mother and a true pioneer of the Old West. But up in her bedroom, away from the trappings of success and maturity, she still kept two dear little teddy bears. The bears, like the woman, were grayed with age but wise with love. And so it is that twin teddy bears raised a child and brightened the darkest night.

Chapter 14

From Rags to Riches

I wonder how many teddy bears end up in trash cans in back alleys or out in front of a building on some busy city street. Many a sad story about a much loved and missing childhood friend might be solved if the youthful owner knew to look in the obvious place. Well-meaning folks sometimes do the strangest things. It may seem just the thing to do to toss a dirty, balding bear into the garbage but such is the stuff of years of pain. An innocent heart can see the value of something loved far past the normal state of beauty.

I once repaired a bear called Rosie whose story, as far as her current owner knew, started in a can of rubbish. Susan's grandfather was a trash collector in the 1950s. One day, as the truck turned into an alley, he thought he saw a large animal peering out from one of the big aluminum waste cans. On closer inspection, the animal turned out to be a big old teddy bear.

The bear was so large that it filled the entire can and Susan's grandfather had to tug at the guy just to free the bear. The surprise was that the bear's legs were missing. This was a three-foot teddy bear even without legs so, before his truck headed down the alley, Grandfather searched the area just hoping that the legs could be found. He thought his grandchildren would get a kick out of hearing the story of the big bear from the alley. Sure enough, stuffed in with other rubbish, the kindly trash collector found one leg, and then the other. The bear spent the rest of the day riding inside the truck as the two men worked the route.

Susan still remembers the first time she saw the teddy. That teddy was a wonder to the little girl who quickly decided to name her Rosie. Susan gave Rosie rides in baby buggies and rocked her in a chair. The trick was to remember to bring the legs along and place them just so. No one ever seemed to be able to reconnect the legs to the bear's body. They were heavy and stuffed with straw. But the child did not care. The bear could still listen and hug and had a dignity that Susan loved.

She sometimes judged her friends by
the way they reacted
to her teddy bear.

As Susan grew, she sometimes judged her friends by the way they reacted to Rosie's predicament. When she was in college, Susan met Pete. Previous boyfriends had suggested that Rosie should be thrown out. What would an almost-grown woman want with a dismembered bear? When Susan took Pete home, he danced the old bear around and asked the teddy to tell him all about little Susy and growing up together. Susan knew she had found her soul mate.

I knew Pete and Susan because they used to come into my shop to buy bears. One day Pete stopped by without Susan. He wanted to surprise her for their anniversary with something she had never seen—Rosie with her legs attached. Could I do it? Well, how could I say no?

Just doing surgery on such a big bear was a challenge. Repairing Rosie was more like auto body repair than fine dressmaking. Her legs had once been jointed but, on close inspection, I realized that the original joints were cardboard. No wonder Rosie had lost her legs. Have you ever canned beans or jelly or tomatoes? If you have, you're familiar with those big, round flat lids that are used for such projects. Rosie has a double set on each side of her hips as joints now. Just for good measure she has fender washers and cotter pins, too.

I would like to tell you that her leg operation was perfect, but it was not. Her legs, though firmly attached, are rather dangly. But Rosie can dance—I mean really, really dance—and her legs can touch the ground.

You get to know a bear when you open them up and perform delicate surgery. As I repaired the close to forty-pound bear, I could see it all so clearly. Rosie was a circus bear, you know, long before Susan and the gentle buggy rides. Just imagine it—a big, smiling bear riding the flying trapeze or performing as a clown's sidekick in the ring. I think that was Rosie's early life. I don't know how she came to be in that trash can. Perhaps the circus left town and their star performer was "retired." Or, maybe a child brought her home to do more tricks in the nursery until Rosie's legs gave way and the nanny tossed the big girl aside for a smaller, easier-to-handle toy. Who knows? But Rosie's lucky day was the day that Susan's grandfather found her there in that alley and took her to a child who would keep her and love her forever.

And Rosie can dance,
I mean really, really
dance

Before I sent Rosie home, I made her a ruffled collar of soft faded burgundy silk. Suddenly, a new gleam appeared in her eyes and you could almost see the circus—the elephants, the man on the flying trapeze. I could almost hear the music. Oh, Rosie will never walk the tightrope again or ride bareback, but she can waltz and warm hearts as only a dear old teddy can.

The last time I saw Rosie was in a picture. She was rocking in a big antique wooden rocker. There is not a hint of her days as second-hand Rose, the girl from the trash bin. No, she is a fine old lady now, sitting in a parlor. Hers is a happy life, for no bear was ever so loved as Rosie.

There are lost bears and there are found bears.
The lost ones have been known to leave big
holes in the hearts of their former owners.
And the found ones, well,
they are the stuff stories are made of
when they are loved and given new life.

Chapter 15

Lost

This story came to me in the year 2001 when computers, e-mail and cellular phones are run-of-the-mill ways to communicate. The truth is I found it in April 2001 while cleaning my garage, but it was dated October 2000. The entire tale had been typewritten on a type of fine, crisp onionskin paper I had not seen for years. It was a miracle that I found it at all. But that misplaced letter somehow fits the story contained within it. I like to think that finding the letter was an omen of good things to come for its writer and that her teddy will be found, too. The mysterious wonder of the whole thing is that both letter and bear were lost in the very same city, decades apart.

When Jean was a little girl, she, her brother and her mother lived in a tiny apartment in Chicago. Her prized possession was an old Steiff bear that had once belonged to her uncle. Although the bear was a hand-me-down toy, he was like new when Jean received him. Her uncle had never played with the teddy because his brothers called it a sissy toy. The little girl loved the bear from the very beginning. Everywhere Jean went, teddy tagged along behind.

As her mother's income increased, Jean's little family of three would move to a larger home. The new place was always on the same bus route—even a child noticed things like that. It was years later that Jean realized that her mother only knew how to get to work one way. So all their homes had to be on that particular bus route.

One move changed Jean's life. It turned her into a searcher and a teddy bear collector.

Every time they moved it seemed something got lost, left behind or forgotten and was never seen again. The day came when teddy could not be found. They went back to the old place, took the same old buses, asked the neighbors but, to the child's sad heart, her beloved teddy bear was gone.

Decades later, Jean is still looking for Teddy. She lives in Los Angeles now but spends every available Saturday searching garage sales for her

As her mother's income increased the little
family of three would move to a larger house.
Something was always lost.

long lost friend. She even has a picture of herself and teddy to compare. Kind of makes you wonder if it wouldn't be a great public service if once a year they ran one of those nationwide milk carton campaigns: "Teddy lost. Last seen in Chicago on bus route 64."

This story took a strange twist a few years ago when Jean received a call from a friend who was settling an estate and then driving across the country to go to auctions and house sales. He asked if there was anything he could find for Jean. Of course there was. Teddy was still missing and Jean sent the man a photo.

Two months had passed when her friend's wife called to invite her to dinner and to see all the things they had found on their trip. Oh, and by the way, "Wait till you see the bear."

Jean's heart raced. What if they had found Teddy? She could hardly stand the delay but was patient as the couple served appetizers. Then there was a long dinner and the "oohing and ahhing" over furniture and china they had acquired.

Finally, the host invited her to come into the living room for coffee and dessert, adding: "I'll get the bear."

"Forget the coffee! Forget the dessert!" her mind screamed. "Just show me the bear!"

At last the host came through the door carrying the bear and Jean's heart felt a quick sense of recognition—Teddy.

Suddenly, the host's wife grabbed the bear and ran toward the bedroom. Jean sadly gathered her coat and purse as she heard them arguing over the teddy.

"But I found it. I love it," one voice insisted.

"We promised it to Jean."

The last she heard the couple was living some place on the East Coast—and that makes two bears that Jean is now missing.

If you are moving; search every corner,
behind every door, from the attic to the cellar.
Don't ever leave a bear behind or you, too, might be
searching, searching

But don't even begin to think that Jean is bear-less. All that searching has produced quite a lot of bears—from a big 1957 Merrythought—the likes of which recently sold for over $1,200 at Christie's Auction House in London—to garage-sale finds. Jean has a gift for recognizing a great bear before anyone else. But then, she has been looking for so many years.

Once in a while I take a bus along Chicago's Michigan Avenue or down State Street. I can't help myself now that I know about Jean's lost bear. I am always looking for an old gray bear tucked into the back corner seat of the bus.

One of Jean's homes was across from Chicago's famous Lincoln Park Zoo and I am considering a trip there, just in case. What if a kindly zookeeper took in the old bear years ago? Where would they put him? Where should I look? I have a wild imagination but what if a lonely gorilla cradled him or he sat on a rail just looking at the tigers until a child found him and took him home? I like it! I'll bet that bear was lost at the zoo. Many are, you know. Jean, have you tried the zoo?

A word to the wise: If you are moving, search every corner, behind every door, from the attic to the basement. Don't ever leave a bear behind or you, too, might be searching, searching for that wonderful little face, those worn paws and the soft friendship of your best loved teddy bear.

It is Saturday morning when I call to check the facts on this story with Jean. The phone rings and rings. I suppose Teddy is still on the loose. And Jean, well, I am just guessing, but she is probably out checking garage sales just in case her old friend has finally moved to the Los Angeles area.

Chapter 16

Big John's Bear

Do you remember your first-grade teacher or the first tree that you climbed? I'll bet you thought your teacher was really, really old and the tree was as tall as the sky. The teacher was probably twenty-something and the tree a mere sapling. I tell you this to say that everything is relative and that memory has a unique way of changing the facts.

There used to be a neighboring merchant who would stop by my shop from time to time. We called him Big John. He had sandy red hair and a full beard. When he stepped through the regulation-size door, he had to duck. Are you getting the picture? We are talking Paul Bunyan here.

Every time he came by he would tell me about his childhood bear and how the bear was so big that he was afraid I could never manage to repair him. Somewhere along the way of playing rough with John, the bear's head had become disconnected from the body. Although he had not seen the bear in many years, John assured me that his mother had kept his childhood buddy.

Over the period of at least two years, whenever John stopped by, he would always tell me the same story. It always ended with a plea for my help in repairing that big bear, if he could get his mother to send it. I had images of needing a piano mover to bring in the bear.

The day came when BIG John ducked his head once more as he walked through my door. It was a bright sunny day and he cast a shadow as he advanced to the counter. His face was all red and strange. I had never seen John like that, so at first I thought something was really wrong. Then he placed a tiny lady's shoebox into my hand.

Now it's time for you to remember what I said about that teacher and the size of that tree. For in my hand was a size 6 lady's shoebox with BIG Ted inside. I admit that his head was unattached but the entire bear was no more than sixteen inches from the top of his teddy ears to the tip of his bear toes.

All I can say is that BIG John is a brave man. A lesser guy would have never brought that tiny bear in after all those years of stories. I guess his desire to fix up his old friend was greater than his fear of momentary embarrassment.

Was the bear just so much a part of John's childhood that he had become larger than life?

Had John grown from a premature baby to a giant of a man? Or was the bear just so much a part of John's childhood that he had become larger than life? I will never really know.

That old bear was the keeper of his master's boyhood games, for when I opened him up, a bit of sand and dirt fell into my lap. His paws and feet were very worn as if he had to work hard to keep up with his little boy. I imagine that Ted did the things boys do from catching bugs to pushing trucks through dirt. How he ever gained the stature in John's mind that he did one can only imagine.

He is the one bear I have repaired that made me feel almost sorry that he was not bigger, better and younger. Somehow, finding him took away an important element of John's childhood memories. His best friend was a bear, just a little teddy bear and not some larger-than-life hero.

I remember having to call a couple of times to get John to stop by to claim his bear, and they seemed a bit awkward with each other. How does such a big guy hold such a tiny bear? The child was gone, gone to a man with the cares of the grown-up world and there was precious little time to think about a childhood toy in John's hectic life. The circle was complete in a way. I would guess that the old bear became a decoration in John's yet-to-be-born child's nursery and the man became more of an adult everyday.

Have you ever driven past your childhood home only to realize how small it was or how low the fence was that you climbed over thinking it was as big as the great wall of China? Then I think you might have a sense of how John felt. Sometimes the owner does discard the bear. They really do. Some people just need to and teddy bears understand. They really do.

Chapter 17

Teddy Bear Collecting and
the $86,000 Anniversary Gift

Collectors and children are the people who keep the hobby of teddy bear collecting alive. There are famous collectors like the Volpps who I will tell you about. There are adults from every walk of life who see the beauty and collectibility of this one hundred year old toy. And today, as it was years ago, children still find kinship with the teddy bear. Oh their methods might be slightly different (read about Jakob and the Internet), but all in all, the teddy bear remains a symbol of love.

Happy Anniversary! Some husbands say it with a card or flowers or dinner and dancing. But in 1987, for their 47th wedding anniversary, Paul Volpp decided he wanted something very special for his wife, Rosemary. They are teddy bear collectors, so what better gift than the beautiful 1926 Steiff bear that he had seen in Sotheby's of London auction catalog? The highest estimate was about $10,000 so Paul, who could not attend, left an open bid.

It seems that Sara Ferguson and the Prince were about to have a child and rumor has it that their agent was also bidding for the bear. The bear named Happy made history that day as the bid went all the way to $86,000. She was the most expensive teddy bear up to that time to sell at auction, although Christie's has since sold a bear for over $120,000.

Rosemary Volpp said she actually felt a little sick when she found out what they had done but she believes that things happen for a reason. Maybe because they were not able to quietly purchase the bear at a more reasonable rate the couple and the bear made national headlines. They decided to turn their newfound notoriety into good. The Volpps and Happy have since raised several hundred thousand dollars for children's hospitals, pediatric aids, Ronald McDonald House, and others.

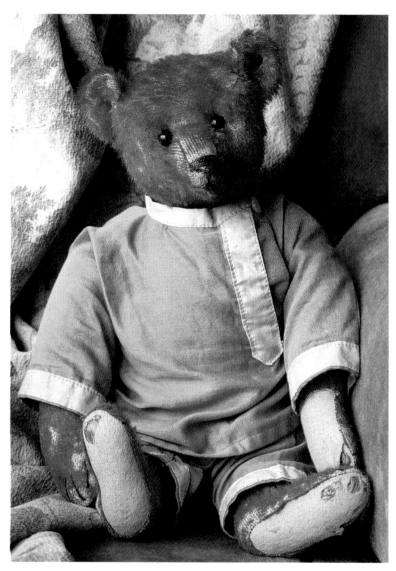

Alfonzo

Purchased for $18,000 by Teddy Bears of Whitney at Christie's in 1989.

Alfonzo once belonged to Princess Xenia, second cousin of Tsar Nicholas of Russia.

The Volpps and their bears have traveled all over the world spreading goodwill through the outstretched paw of a teddy and the loving hearts of two caring Americans.

For one elementary school teacher turned teddy bear collector, the journey toward America and our most loved toy started in April 30, 1975 when a boy and his mother left their country on the last day they would have a chance at freedom. Ho Phi Le and his mother fled Vietnam that spring day over twenty-five years ago to what he calls, "this amazing country—America, a land of opportunity and the greatest people in the world."

Hardships notwithstanding, Ho calls himself a lucky, lucky guy who was born and raised with love. For Mr. Le, as it is with many of us who love this toy-turned-collectible, the teddy bear is about basic love, and a simpler time. The bears remind us of the old days. Life, like a good old bear, is about love. And love and teddy bears go on and on.

I have heard of several teddy bears being the focal point during natural childbirth or being used to win someone's heart. I once knew of a man who ruined an Armani suit trying to save a bear he saw floating off the coast of California. The bear made it. The suit pants didn't. The bear now, living on dry land, goes by the name of Davy Jones.

Today the Internet plays a big role in this changing world. But teddy bears are taking over the Net, too. There are over 10,000 web sites that focus on teddy bears and I think that is barely (no pun intended) scratching the surface.

In perusing the Net, one of my favorite finds was Jakob, a seven-year-old boy from Denmark who collects teddy bears. He tells of having sixteen bears in his collection. I love the section where he talks about his newest teddy bear named Blop Baloo. This modern kid couldn't decide on a name for his teddy so he "asked several Internet newsgroups and got lots of good suggestions." But the one both he and his teddy liked the most was Blop Baloo. And so it is the 21st Century and children are surfing the Net to get help in naming their teddy bears. Wow. What would Margarete Steiff say?

Chapter 18

Moving West

I think it was Winnie-the-Pooh who said something like, "If you live to be a hundred, I want to live to be a hundred minus one day, so I never have to live without you." And so it is with people who love so deeply. It is a hard reality to spend years searching for a lost childhood friend. Or is it the very innocence of the time that we are searching for? Who knows, but we are all searching for people and things left along the way.

Picture the family standing out in front of the house. The moving van is packed. The children and animals are in the station wagon when, suddenly, one child sprints from the back seat to search one more time for her missing and much loved companion, her teddy bear.

They have to go. It is thousands of miles to California but the child will not leave the house. Finally, the mother admits that she burned the teddy with other rubbish. And the tears begin to flow. The sobs from the back of that old wagon carried with them a feeling of great loss, and the sadness of leaving hangs heavy in the air. For a long time there is only the sound of the soft sobs and the pavement stretching before them. They cannot go back. Actions and decisions have been made. Good-byes have been said. But for that child the lost bear will always be searched for and revisited in her memories.

Doris makes teddy bears now. Maybe it is to fill that hole in her heart. Ask her if she had a teddy bear when she was a girl and you can hear the sweet memories in her voice. It's a funny thing, she last saw that bear in 1949 when she was ten or eleven years old, but she can describe him in great detail. He was a mohair bear (soft wool plush) and his color was an unusual mustard-gold. He stood thirteen or fourteen inches tall with a body that was kind of football-shaped and legs that were jointed with wire. He had straight little arms. But the most important thing about him was that he had such a kind face.

Doris is still looking for that face. Search though she may, she has never seen that face again. But she is sure that someday she will find one of his kinfolk.

Doris was the middle child and after her brother's birth she felt all alone, somehow, left out. So her teddy was her best friend and companion. He was so loved that all his fur was worn off and her mother had mended his paws several times with the materials from Doris' old heavy, tan cotton stockings. It just never entered Doris' mind that she would ever have to go on without that bear.

Doris' normally cheerful voice catches as she tells the story. She can still just hear her mother saying, "Such foolishness, such foolishness." Ten years old and she still needed that worn-out old bear. Those were the days before

It just never entered her mind that she

popular psychology was a household subject, so her mother could not know what it would mean to Doris. She still cannot believe that Teddy was burned and left in Pennsylvania, but it is true.

Doris lives in a tiny town in southern California, now, and she has children and grandchildren of her own. She made her first teddy bear as a gift for one of her grandchildren. She even owns a teddy bear shop. But Doris is still searching for one special bear to replace the one she lost when her family moved over fifty years ago. He had such a sweet, gentle face, you know, and hundreds of bears later she has never seen one quite like him.

would have to go on without the bear

Chapter 19

Love Stories

Now, Neiman Marcus was not his usual haunt. In fact, shopping was not really his idea of a good time until he was sent from the firehouse to check out the fire safety at one of San Francisco's most prestigious retail establishments. It was just a routine inspection. He and a couple of other guys would be in and out in no time, or so Don thought until he saw a certain young lady behind one of the cosmetic counters. Nothing could have forewarned him that he was about to become a Neiman Marcus regular.

Why the very next day or was it that afternoon, he was back there trying to get the girl's name. Every day off, Don visited that cosmetic counter, but try as he might with candy, flowers, and charm, the woman would not go out with him.

This could be a tale of woe if it were not for a teddy bear. Just when the fireman was about to give up he happened upon Bears To Go. Now, one thing is for certain, humans will tell total strangers things that they don't share with their friends. I remember him well — tall, very handsome, and at his wits end as to how to get a date with the object of this affections. When he shared with me that he was trying to get a woman that he had met to go out with him to no avail, my first thought was that she must be crazy. Instead, I suggested that he try a teddy bear.

Well, need I tell you more? Doris fell for the bear. A date was arranged and before I knew it, every time I looked up, Don was there for another teddy bear. A year or so later, a teddy bear even helped Don purpose marriage to Doris. Then there was a tiny bear for her bridal bouquet, and a great, big bear and flowers for the day their first child was born.

The truth is that I never met Doris, but the sparkle in Don's eyes told it all when he spoke of his beloved wife. The last time that I saw my fireman friend, he was pushing a baby carriage.

Teddy bears are skilled at carrying the
message of love from
one heart to another.

He had stopped by to introduce the Bear Lady to his new baby and of course, to buy that child the best bear in the store.

Teddy bears are very skilled at carrying the message of love from generation to generation and from one heart to another. One of my friends used to tell a story of a lost bear found and how it made her parents fall in love. It seems that, during their early courtship, Sally's father would take her mother to the city park. One day, as they approached a familiar oak tree, they both saw—almost at the same time—a teddy bear sitting in the shade of the big arms of a tree. It was as if the bear had been on a picnic and was left behind by a forgetful child or a haggard nanny. Sally's mother fell in love with her young suitor when she saw the care with which he lifted the bear.

They took the bear home and for weeks returned as often as they could with the bear, looking for the owner and stealing a kiss while Teddy put his paws over his eyes or wisely looked at a bird in the tree. How could a girl not love a guy who would take her and a forlorn teddy bear for walks through the local park?

The owner never came to claim the bear but, year after year, from courtship to marriage to children and grandchildren, that bear found so many years earlier in a local park has brought joy and wonder to Sally's parents and their children. As he makes his yearly appearance under their Christmas tree, they always wonder where his original owner could be and marvel at how lucky they were to find such a wise, gentle, and enduring creature.

Chapter 20

A Noble Companion

*"In the world of toys, the teddy bear is King Arthur—incapable of
an unkind or mean thought, courageous, and gallant."*
John Darcy Noble

For as long as he could remember, Teddy was John Darcy Noble's companion. Teddy saw him through the measles, through his school years and then on to art school. When John was called up to go to World War II, he learned that he could not enlist in the military. So, he became a firefighter in his home country of England. The war was not some distant affair. The bombs dropped daily and people's lives were forever changed.

John wore a big-pocketed raincoat to his job and was often called upon to risk his own life to save the occupants from the flames of a burning building. He had a secret, though. Teddy came right along with him, traveling from one scene of carnage to the next. From deep inside that oversized pocket, Teddy gave his lifelong friend the courage and the grit to help with one disaster after the other.

Now, Teddy was no longer beautiful in the classic teddy bear way. By the time he was a fireman's assistant, he was missing one ear and was blind. But, like all good teddies, he still had his heart.

Teddy was also an old hand at heated situations. When John contracted measles as a child, his mother baked the bear in the oven for a while to kill the germs before Teddy could rejoin his friend.

As John puts it, "I adored him so." And so there they were, the battered and loved old bear and the young English man, battling the ravages of war-torn Britian. Then one night John recalls a particularly bad fire with people inside calling for help. The fire was so intense that John removed his coat and put it aside in order to get to a woman trapped under burning rubble. Just as he brought her to safety the building collapsed. Like the very people he had

For as long as he could remember,
Teddy was his companion,
through measles,
school, and . . .

saved, John lost something very dear to him that night. The occupants' belongings where reduced to ashes, and John stood by helpless as his dear teddy went with them.

Tonight, somewhere in England, Teddy is part of the earth that makes London the home of great theater, royal princesses and beautifully romantic gardens. In America, a much older man's eyes fill with a liquid twinkle when he tells me about a bear he carries in his heart and once called just "Teddy."

"He was a real hero, you know," he tells me.

Moving on from the bittersweet story of Teddy, John tells me the story of a nun who had her childhood bear into her 80s. Her story contains a much brighter ending for a loyal teddy bear. But I know if Teddy were here today, he would be so proud. He'd want to tell John, "Good job. I trained you to have the caring soul of a teddy bear and to be able to give up something you really love for the good of your fellow man."

Chapter 21

The Nun's Story

There was a nun by the name of Sister Kadmon. It seems she entered the convent when she was very young and was, to all who watched her progress, a model nun. Sister Kadmon was in a "closed order" and had not spoken for years, but late on the night before she was to take her final vows she journeyed the darkened halls of the convent until she came to the door of her Mother Superior.

With great regret she told the Mother Superior that she could not take her final vows the next day. Though she had taken the vows of poverty, and had given up everything she owned all those years ago, as a novice she had kept one possession. Now, she realized that nothing could make her give up her one last belonging, her teddy bear. That bear had been smuggled into the convent on the day she arrived. The faithful nun had come at the eleventh hour asking for dispensation to keep teddy or to tell the Mother that she must leave the nunnery.

So great was the promise of Sister Kadmon and her value as a nun that she was given that dispensation and it is said that she slept with her bear each night until she was 80. As an elderly woman she became worried about what would happen to her bear when she died. She requested that teddy either be buried with her or be given to a younger nun. Both requests were denied and the good sister was left with the dilemma of what to do with her one worldly treasure. Today, Sister Kadmon's beloved teddy bear resides at the Museum of the City of New York for all to see.

Chapter 22

A Few Good Deeds

To ease loneliness and inspire love through an
ageless symbol of love, the teddy bear.
Good Bears of the World motto

Each year Good Bears of the World gives over 20,000 teddy bears to children and seniors. Good Bears of the World was founded in 1969 by James T. Ownby, a broadcast executive from Hawaii. He was inspired by a story he had heard about Russell McLean of Lima, Ohio. It seems that Mr. McLean got the idea to give teddy bears to children in the hospital and around Lima he was known as the teddy bear man.

Long after visiting hours were over and the rooms were dark and lonely, the sick children of Lima and the surrounding area had a bear paw to hold because of Russell's thoughtfulness. Being a teddy bear lover himself, Jim Ownby, thought that Mr. McLean's idea could be expanded on to help children and seniors in all sorts of stressful situations. So Jim Ownby dedicated much of his life to promoting and financing the great works of Good Bears of the World.

To this day Good Bears of the World, an organization of volunteers now based in Toledo, Ohio, provides teddy bears to children of all ages, where love, solace and comfort can make a difference. The teddies go to victims of floods, tornadoes, hurricanes, and domestic violence. The bears continue to be given to the sick, injured and to underprivileged children and senior citizens. Good Bears provides teddy bears to fire and police departments, psychologists and grief counselors across the nation and the world.

A Good Bear member tells of taking a little teddy to a nursing home and giving it to an elderly resident there. Each time the member would visit she noticed that the bear's nose was getting more and more worn. She finally offered to bring the bear's owner a new bear or to repair the damaged one. "Oh no, he got this way from kissing." Who would want a replacement for such a love worn companion? And the bear rode off in a mesh bag that hung from the front of the lady's walker. Beauty is only fur deep, you know.

Chapter 23

One Hundred Years of the Teddy Bear
1902-2002

In America if something has been around for one hundred years, it is considered to be an antique. So teddy bears are antiques, or at least some of them are. Those early bears had humped little backs, long arms and black shoe-button eyes. They were patterned after real bears, and if you study the anatomy of real bruins, you will see the resemblance.

The wonderful thing about teddy bears is that they are as fresh today as they were one hundred years ago. They are much-loved children's toys. But they are, in many ways, a fashion statement, too. They have gone from long arms and humped backs in the early 1900s to googlie-eyed, short-armed fellows in the 1950s to a wide range today.

The wonderful qualities of gentleness and unconditional love that teddy bears exude seem to make them timeless. For everyone from your grandmother to your grandchildren, they are a classic. Teddy bears come in every imaginable shape, size and color. The facade is not what matters so much in a bear. It is what they stand for—gentleness, childhood and love that never fails. Teddy bears have journeyed all over this globe from the Titanic to backyard baby carriages.

So loved is the teddy bear that the hobby of collecting them actually has a name. The hobby is called arctophily (the collecting of teddy bears).

If you'd like to know if your fondness for teddy bears qualifies you to be called an arctophile, just take this simple test:

I. When you look at a teddy bear, you . . .
    A. Feel cuddly all over.
    B. Think about a brake job on you car.
    C. Wonder whether you have paid your telephone bill.

II. After reading in TV Guide that Winnie-the-Pooh is appearing on a television special you . . .
    A. Get yourself a bowl of popcorn and plop in front of your television, "bearly" able to contain yourself.
    B. Read a good book dealing with the migration of aardvarks.
    C. Turn the radio on to "Car Talk."

III. When you see a perfectly good teddy bear on the side of the road as you commute to work one morning you . . .
    A. Try, but soon realize you cannot safely cross three lanes of traffic to rescue the poor fellow (but the scene flashes through your mind several times that day).
    B. Wish people wouldn't toss things from windows. If makes your city look too messy.
    C. Make a joke about a bear on the side of the road and e-mail it to three friends.

Okay, so turn the book upside down and see if you are an arctophile.

If you answered all the questions in the "A" category, resign yourself. You are infected with a highly contagious disease that is said to affect nearly everyone who comes in contact with a teddy bear.

Teddy bear collecting is a bridge. Maybe all collecting is the connection to our past, to things that we loved, or objects that were saved by people that we can only dream about.

Teddy bears have an almost universal appeal. Humans seem to bond easily with a bear. We love their cuddly nature and seem to just expect to receive love from them. Psychologists have long known that people need to hold and to be held. Ask any teddy bear lover and they will tell you that a good bear is a great hugger and maybe that is part of the attraction.

Police departments, hospitals, trauma centers, and fire departments started in the 1980s and 1990s to enlist the help of teddy bears to calm and care for the people that they serve. The tradition continues to this very day.

We may never understand the complex set of circumstances that enables a simple stuffed toy to provide so much comfort and joy. It simply is a fact and maybe that is enough. Some of the most important things in life just are. It is teddy bear's destiny to be loved and to return love to the human heart that is open.

Chapter 24

Where Teddy Bears Come From

There are basically two ways that teddy bears are born. Either they are made by manufacturing companies or handmade by artists around the world. In the United States as interest in nostalgic collectibles and antiques grew, teddy bears could be seen coming down from the attics and out of dusty old trunks to climb onto display shelves. These child-loved and well worn old friends inspired a new generation of teddy bear artists to try their hand at making unique patterns and styles of bears. The teddy bear show was born and adults from across the globe began in earnest to collect teddy bears. The early 1980s actually saw a new commercial enterprise emerged—handmade teddy bears as a business and livelihood for their creators.

The teddy bear makers/artists created one-of-a-kind collectible teddy bears for a mostly adult market. The interest and the artists continue to this day. Their styles are as diverse as all other forms of art and each creation reflects the skill, interest, and inspiration of the artist. I could write a whole book on the many teddy bear artists in America and around the world.

A teddy bear can be made of almost any fabric or material. Over the years, several people have told me stories of making a teddy bear from a favorite old coat that belonged to a deceased loved one. One of my favorite stories was of a customer who's father had owned a dog-earred old London Fog trenchcoat. She described it as one of those saggy, beige, much worn Detective Columbo sort of topcoats. It just spoke of her father so rather than toss his signature coat, she zipped out the alpaca lining and had two little teddy bears made of the wooly brown material that had so long kept her father warm.

Although factory-made teddy bears such as those from Steiff, Hermann, Gund, and others are often talked about, I thought you would like to hear the stories of a few unique teddy bear artists. There are actually hundreds of teddy bear makers in America today and the number changes and grows daily. I'll tell you about four.

Catherine Bordi was one of the first teddy bear artists that I ever met and befriended. Her early bears, created in a little cabin in the deep forests of northern California, seemed to carry the wholesomeness and goodness of the woodland creatures and the optimism of their youthful creator. Catherine's little cubs, like all artist made teddy bears, were born one at a time. I remember well the excitement that I felt when we first met—the bear artist and the shopkeeper. We shared this kindred spirit, this sense that teddy bears have souls and are about goodness and gentleness.

The materials for making teddy bears was scarce in the early 1980s so Cathy set about to find the source of European quality plush with which to hand make her creations.

"When I finally identified the companies, I had so much fun pretending to be a big toy company myself," she explains. "I figured I had a better chance at getting them to export to me." Catherine says she signed her letters with different titles like Marketing Director, Director of Design and Materials, and Manager. "I lived in fear that they would call me and hear my dog barking in the background," she laughs, " but they never did."

I never realized until I interviewed Cathy for this book how much she had built up her company's status to the European fabric vendors. That might explain why, when I traveled to meet one vendor in the early 1980s, that the entire town was anticipating my visit. I felt a little like Dorothy being welcomed to Lollipop Land. The folks at the factory actually rolled out a red carpet for me. There I was, the owner of two tiny teddy bear stores and the mayor of a British town as well as the mohair factory owner and his entire staff were waiting for me at the top of the stairs. I remember thinking that I had to order enough mohair to save an entire town. We were all pretty young then.

Beverly Port is unquestionably the Mother of Modern Teddy Bear Art. As early as the 1950s, Beverly had begun to design and create stuffed toys that would become the bridge between manufactured toy bears and the modern age of soft sculpture bears created as originals for collectors of art and teddy bears. She describes the purpose of her work as bringing out that sleeping child that lives within every adult.

Beverly's two children, John and Kimberlee, have followed in her footsteps. All are accomplished teddy bear artists, writers, teddy bear consultants and honored guests and speakers at teddy bear functions all over the world.

Playing with one of her mom's handmade
teddy bears, Jennifer Bordi is carrying on a
family tradition

Teddy bears have always been a part of Catherine Bordi's family life. Pictured here is her mother, uncle, and grandmother on an outing with the family teddy in the 1930s.

Teddy artist at work.

Beverly calls her bears Time Machine Teddies and in that vain did a series of teddy bears for one of my early catalogs that I always loved. The bears were called Scraps and each was decorated with unique buttons from her mother's old button box. In that one teddy — the new and the old — come together to create two generations of love..

From their Midwestern homes, or as Etta calls it, "a small prison town near Chicago," Pat Joho and Etta Foran were among the first bear artists to travel all over America carrying their wares to teddy bear collector shows. When the modern movement was just getting its wings, they were like teddy bears themselves—two wide-eyed innocents giving humor and goodness to a world that would later become very competitive.

A simple Christmas gift from Etta to Pat started the teddy bear adventure for them. Seems Pat never had a bear as a child. One thing lead to another and the two decided to travel to Ohio to see what a teddy bear show/event was all about. "It was a big deal, the first time either of us had left our husbands for a weekend," Etta says. "I saw my first artist-made bear there and all the way home I told Pat that I wanted us to make a bear."

Although Pat kept assuring Etta that they could do it, Etta had her doubts. She is not your classic Martha Stewart type. Her mother bailed her out of high school sewing class. Etta claims that her first bear looked more like a shark. Nonetheless, she says, "I am proof that if you want something badly enough you can do it. We just kept at it."

To hear these two tell their bear tales is to understand the chasing of the American Dream. They even found a unique and free setting to photograph their bears. While everyone else was photographing their teddy bears with honey, flowers, and such, this pair discovered day old pies.

That is how they wound up at Baker's Square (a restaurant that specializes in pie) after closing one night when it was robbed at gunpoint. "I often wonder what those robbers thought," she says. "There was the clean-up crew and two women in bowling shirts trying to make photographs of bears and old pies. It's a wonder they didn't shoot us." They did wind up being locked in the walk in freezer with what they describe as a hundred frozen apple pies and a claustrophobic Vietnam Vet. I think the bears stayed outside.

Beverly Port's Time Machine Teddies

*This one is called Scraps and is decorated
with buttons from her mother's treasured sewing box.*

Hey, you could freeze to death in there.

Seymour Eaton wrote some of the earliest teddy bear stories about two real bears who find their way out of the deep Colorado woods. The Roosevelt Bears slap-sticked and bumbled their way across the country. Pat and Etta attacked teddy bear making with that same wide-eyed wonder.

And their stories led to many happy endings. Pat and Etta's bears were eventually included in the exhibit at the Incorporated Gallery on Madison Avenue in New York in 1987, the Bears To Go catalog and in calendars and teddy bear books. In 1994, Ashton-Drake Galleries discovered one of Pat and Etta's bears, Benjamin, and for several years the team designed bears for the company.

These two funny ladies have some serious talent and Etta continues to design and make teddy bears. They may have been the first artists to ever use pellets in the bodies of their bears to create a soft, floppy toy.

To understand the teddy bear collector market you would have to be familiar with similar collectibles and collector shows. There are collector shows for everything from vintage clothing to Star Wars memorabilia. The Internet has changed the face of collecting today but in the early eighties well through the 1990s, if you wanted to make handmade teddy bears, one of the best sources for selling your creations was at events held all over the United States.

And so it is . . . teddy bears come in many forms, can be manufactured or made one at a time in a home or artist workshop . . . the message is the same. Teddy bears are toys designed to bring out the fun, love, and gentle enjoyment of childhood.

*Clyde by
Pat Joho and
Etta Foran*

LITTLE
KITTEN
SERIES

The Story
of THE THREE BEARS

Chapter 25

The Literature that Started It All

The moment I unpack and put Theodore on my bedside table
with his friends and props, the strange place becomes a kind of home.
I think he is a symbol of unloneliness.
Peter Bull
(speaking at Teddy Tribune
Convention 1984)

When I was very young, my Grandmother Greene (MaAnnie) and I
had a little ritual we practiced whenever I spent the night at her house. In
the morning I would pad barefoot into her warm, fragrant kitchen for
homemade biscuits with fresh churned butter and her best berry jam. She
would look up and ask me what I dreamed about. "The Three Little Bears,"
I would always answer. She would laugh and hug me. It would be safe to say
that from an early age, I was influenced and warmed by teddy bear literature.

I won't recount for you the familiar old tales of The Three Little Bears, The
Teddy Bear's Picnic, Paddington, or Winnie-the-Pooh, but they are all part
of the nostalgia and kinship with teddy bears that touches many an adult's
heart. I think the day I read Winnie-the-Pooh aloud to my late husband was
the day he fell in love with me, but that is a whole other story . . . "The
Power of Pooh."

In the early 1980s, there were several books that influenced the way people
would view and value teddy bears. But the movement really got its start in
1969 when British actor Peter Bull decided to declare his devotion to teddy
bears in The Teddy Bear Book.

Beginning with the foreword Peter tells a story of woe, of a destroyed teddy
bear, and of a life-changing evening that he spent with fellow grown-ups
sharing teddy bear trauma stories. In this social gathering of friends and
acquaintances he suddenly realized that he was not the only adult with a
teddy bear secret. The Teddy Bear Book that ensued was the catalyst that
spurred an entire generation to collect, preserve and revere teddy bears—
and to seek out like-minded humans.

Mr. Bull's book is the sort of book you read on a cold, rainy afternoon while sipping tea. Suddenly, you no longer feel like an alien in this adult world. Through his book you realize that you are not alone. One by one arctophiles from around the globe began to step up and be counted. Serious teddy bear collections started to take shape and bears crowded bookshelves, rode in briefcases, and became an acceptable adult collectible. In many ways, it was Peter Bull who helped the teddy bear find a new home outside of the nursery.

Peter Bull and Aloysius
with guest bear

Another ground-breaking book and, to this day, one of the best histories of the teddy bear is Pat Schoonmaker's *A Collector's History of the Teddy Bear* published in 1981 by Hobby House Press. Pat's exhaustive search of the Library of Congress records gives us so much of the commercial history of the teddy bear fad that started in 1903.

The book that still makes my heart sing whenever I have the time to wander through its beautiful pages is *My Circle of Bears* by Michele Durkson Clise published in 1981 by Green Tiger Press. I will never forget the first time I read the book and studied the beautiful pictures. Finally, I had found another soul who saw meaning in a magic world of well-worn old teddy bears, bits of antique lace and a vivid imagination. Ms. Clise's collection of bears lived the romantic life I could only dream of—shopping trips to Paris, lounging as "regulars" at a local bistro, or sleeping in beds of down and lavender.

Finally, let me circle back to Mr. Bull. When all is said and done, it was Peter Bull who first made adults of my generation feel that it was okay to think about teddy bears, collect teddies and to see teddy bears as real somehow.

I remember the first time I met Peter Bull, he asked me to join him for tea. And I recall the last time I ever saw him, too. It was a cold February day in New York City as he disappeared into a crowded street. He was carrying his big old bear, Aloysius. Peter waved the bear's paw at me in a silent "Good-bye." As he walked away, I saw him reach into his coat pocket— I will always believe—to touch his longtime companion, Theodore.

Whenever I had seen Peter over the years, he always knew me by name, knew we had bears in common and, on several occasions, asked me to give Aloysius a little repair. I never thought of him as a famous actor but as a fellow teddy bear lover. Peter, like the writers who followed, add their own echo to the sentiment pinned to that famous little waif bear, Paddington: "Please look after this bear."

Teddy bears have been lending us a loving ear, a paw to hold and a soft chest to cry into for at least a century. It just took a few brave writers to remind our rusty hearts of the gentleness of these lovely childhood friends.

TEDDY-G

TO BE CALLED FOR

LOST & FOUND
DEP'T
(Found on Aisle A
2.32 P.M.

No Remarks

FOUND
IN
HAT DEP'T

TO BE CALLED FOR

LOST

Chapter 26

Famous Teddy Bear Favorites

Paddington Bear

Dressed in bright galoshes, a big mackintosh and floppy hat, a little bear (about 9 years old) bravely leaves his Aunt Lucy and his home in deepest, darkest Peru only to be lost on a platform at London's Paddington Station. "Please Look After this Bear," the tag around his neck read when the Brown's (Mr. and Mrs. Brown, to be exact) found him wandering, looking forlorn and lost.

Thus enters one of the most famous literary teddy bear figures of all times—Paddington Bear. It is interesting to note that Michael Bond, the author who created the Paddington Bear stories, was a writer who had always worked on stories of adult interest. At the time he wrote the first story about Paddington he had no idea he would become a very famous children's book author.

It seems that one day while cutting through Selfridge's, one of England's largest department stores, he purchased a lone little bear that he spotted sitting askew on a shelf in the toy department. Mr. and Mrs. Bond lived near Paddington Station so upon arriving home, Michael began a story about a bear called Paddington. The stories were written as a gift for his wife and for his own amusement.

Michael says that one of the great beauties of Paddington is that he is forever frozen at that age of wonder and eternal newness—9 years old. Now, this happy marmalade lover did not find instant success. The first Paddington book went to six publishers before it was finally taken and published. Mr. Bond recalls meeting, quite by accident, Peggy Fortnum, the illustrator, who would help give form and visual identity to Paddington Bear. Gabrielle Design in England made the first plush Paddington bears.

Next time you are at the train station or on a boat traveling to or from deepest darkest Peru, watch out for a little bear wearing a tag that reads: "Please Look After this Bear." If you take him home, beware that he is only 9 years old, into everything and always hungry for marmalade.

Winnie-the-Pooh

By the early 1920s, Alan Alexander Milne was one of the most successful, prolific and best-known playwrights in all of England. His first big hit was a play called "Mr. Pim Passes By." He was also a novelist with several successful novels written during this same period.

On August 21, 1920, Christopher Robin Milne was born. Alan wrote "Vespers" after watching Christopher say his evening prayers one night and gave it to his wife, Daphne, as a gift. He told her she could keep all the money she could get for publishing it. After it was printed in the January 1923 issue of Vanity Fair, "Vespers" became an instant success and Milne was asked to provide another children's verse for a new children's magazine. That poem was "The Dormouse and the Doctor" and it also quickly became famous.

In 1926, Mr. Milne would write a little book of short stories about the toys in Christopher Robin's nursery that was to change his destiny forever. The book was entitled Winnie-the-Pooh and, once again, the book was an instant commercial success. In all, A. A. Milne wrote four books in the Pooh series. They are: When We Were Very Young, Winnie-the-Pooh, Now We Are Six (1927) and, finally, House at Pooh Corner (1928).

The two great ironies of Milne's life were that the son he wrote so lovingly about appears to have been somewhat estranged from his father and the very success he enjoyed with his children's stories unwittingly changed A. A. Milne's fate. After Winnie-the-Pooh, Milne never again enjoyed his earlier success as a playwright and prominent figure in the London theatre world.

In 1952, A. A. Milne suffered a stroke and was left bedridden until his death in 1956. In 1961 his wife Daphne sold the film rights to Disney who gave new faces to the beloved characters from The Hundred Acre Woods.

Not long ago I was in New York City on a business trip. I seem to always be rushing these days. As I hurried passed a branch of the New York Public Library, I noticed a poster of the most famous bear of all time, Winnie-the-Pooh. I couldn't help but pause to look at that picture. I decided to take a moment to go inside and view the real Pooh. (I've noticed that, as an adult, I take far too few breaks to enjoy the miracles that are around every corner.) There he was—a beautiful, child-loved bear with his partners in adventure surrounding him. Piglet was so tiny and almost flat from wear, Kanga was missing Roo, and I can't remember whether or not Tigger had his tail.

All these years I had hurried passed the original Pooh crew and never stopped just to meet the plush toys that inspired one of the best-loved children's stories of all time. For a moment I stood in the second floor of that New York City library and I was a child just stopping by to say, "Hello, Pooh." The visit did this adult heart good.

Was it Christopher Robin or was it Pooh who asked the other to always remember them? Whichever way it goes, there once was a little boy and a bear, and their adventures have touched so many of our lives. The bear now lives at the library in New York. And the boy, well, the story really isn't about the boy, now, is it?

The Roosevelt Bears

In the early 1900s, the close association of President Roosevelt with bears inspired writer Seymour Eaton to create the Roosevelt Bears. Working with illustrator, R. K. Culver, Eaton invented two bears: Teddy B and Teddy G. The first Roosevelt Bear book was published in 1906 under the title, The Roosevelt Bears, Their Travels and Adventures. Now, the Roosevelt bears are clearly not cute toy bears, they are giant bears from the Colorado backwoods. Through the magic of story telling, these two wander into civilization dressed in human clothes and mingle with the common and not so common folk.

Eaton is often credited with being the first writer to use the name "Teddy." Now least you finish this book thinking that B is for bad and G is for good, let me tell you the real story. Teddy G actually stood for gray and gay, and Teddy B for black and brave. This traveling duo entertained their readers with tales of adventure from train rides to repairing automobiles — all a novelty in the early 1900s.

The
Roosevelt
Bears

Chapter 27

Faded Photographs

In my mind, I live in a beautiful, gentle world. My lifelong love of beautiful things from a bygone time is evident in the objects that I save and collect. I am keenly interested in understanding why a certain old teddy bear was saved or who the person was who smiles back at me from a faded old photograph. When I touch the soft fabric of a dress worn so long ago or look into the eyes of a child on a faded picture postcard, I feel drawn to that time and that person. The dust of which I am made has mixed with theirs, and I long to know their stories. I am a seeker and a time traveler.

Have you ever lost something that you really, really wanted to keep forever . . . a picture, an old letter, a birthday check? You search high and low. You have moved thousands of miles from where you last saw the object of your frustration. You can just see the lost object, but year after year you search and you can't find it. When it comes to mind you look again, probably in the same places and you say a little prayer to the air or the walls or whatever and hope it magically appears. Such is the case with Jessie Pratt.

It was on my birthday in 1986 when I first laid eyes on Jessie, a hauntingly beautiful little child holding onto a teddy bear and looking up at me from an old sepia tone picture postcard. I was in an antique store with my husband. I was up to my usual — looking through every old photographs for pictures of children with teddy bears. There she was the quintessential Victorian girl with her bear. A picture is worth a thousand words and this one clearly shows a bond between that child and that bear that said it all for me. The bear was her protector, friend, and confidant and vice versa.

I purchased the postcard and took Jessie home with me. And the movies of mine ran full speed. Jessie was the star of a childhood movie about a rich little girl who needed that bear. They seemed like such buddies in that old photo. I liked Jessie so much that I took the original and had a huge poster made of the pair for my shop. They were the poster children

The dust of which I am made is mixed with theirs,
and I long to know their stories

When I touch the soft fabric of a dress worn
so long ago or look into the eyes of a child
on a faded picture postcard, I feel drawn to
that time and that person.

for the teddy bear movement. Every display that I was asked to do, from museum to convention, a poster of Jessie and her bear traveled with my antiques teddies.

So how did I lose the original? My life got so complex, I closed my store, and then I moved thousands of miles from Berkeley, California to Chicago, Illinois. Still about every six months on a Saturday I search for Jessie. Where is that little picture? It matters because I want to show it to you. You would love her too, and you would see what I mean about that child and that bear.

How do I include this story in this book without her picture? I just need you to work with me on this one. Jessie is wearing a little white Victorian dress and the bear that she is holding faces her as if he needs reassurance, and there is a slight tilt of the head or something about the way she holds the bear. I can't explain it, but Jessie loved that bear. She is so serious and worried and the bear seems the same. Maybe she reminds me of me, serious, and a believer in the goodness of teddy bears.

Well, actually there is more to the story. About a year after I found the first photo of Jessie, I was back in the same little town in Northern California but in a different antique store. You guessed it; I was searching through pictures again. This time my husband noticed a woman in her thirties or forties holding a worn little teddy. Before he turned it over, he matter of factly told me, "That is your Jessie and her bear." Believe it or not on the back in pencil it says, "Just me and Teddy – Jessie Pratt." How had the beautiful little girl in the fine clothes become this woman in black standing near what seemed like a shack? And the second picture confirmed what I always knew; Jessie did love that teddy. After all those years she still had Teddy. Oh, he looked smaller in her grown-up hands and he no longer faced the camera. The contrast was startling – the young Jessie so beautiful with long curls, soft white dress, and proud Teddy and years later Jessie in a course black dress, chopped off hair, and Teddy. Was Teddy the last possession of her childhood? Was she happy? I see no ring on her fingers. Could it be true that in the end it was just Jessie and Teddy?

If I ever find that picture of Jessie it will be in my next book. I feel like I carry them in my heart, the child and the bear and the woman that grew up to live with her childhood teddy bear.

The last time I saw that photo of Jessie it was in an envelope tacked to the wall of my stock room at the teddy bear store in Berkeley. That was years and years ago, I ask myself, is it possible that I moved and left Jessie in that closet? Why do old photos get left behind anyway? All I can say is there was once a little child who had a teddy bear and I saw the proof of their love in the image of an old photograph. And the child and the bear grew up and stayed together. Many people have told me stories about being In Search of Teddy, but I search for the child, that gentle child in all of us.

My only remaining shot of Jessie as a child. Look in the upper left corner of the picture. That's Jessie and Teddy.

Just me and Teddy,
Jessie Pratt

Chapter 28

Valentine

In the early 1980s, I spoke at a senior citizen's gathering about teddy bears and what they mean to me. An elderly gentleman kept talking loudly over my speech, but teddy bears have taught me a sense of patience and kindness so I muddled on somehow. When everyone else had left, the loud talker remained.

"I never had a teddy bear, you know,"
he informed me.
"I was too old for one when they came in."
That was hard for me to believe at first until he told me
that his name was Valentine,
and that he had been born on
Valentine's Day 1880.
The day he spoke with me he was 104 years old.

"Wish I had had a teddy bear,"
he said,
"might have made me more of a dreamer."
He continued,
"You are a dreamer, girlie.
And life has a way of making you let go of your dreams,
never let go of your dreams."

When I took my leave, Valentine finally had his bear. The trouble is it might have been a little late because he seemed awkward and not sure what to do with it as a little tear gathered in the corner of his eye. He even tried to give it to a lady who stood nearby, but she thankfully insisted that Valentine take the bear with him.

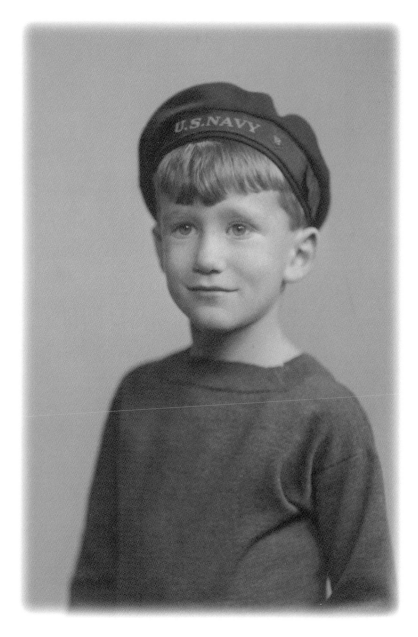

He actually remembered seeing ads for the newest toy in town, the teddy bear.

He never had one till he was 104.

As for me, I walked carefully from that place, so as not to jar the dreams from my heart. That was so many years ago and I am sure that Valentine has left this earth. But I will always remember the man who cautioned me about dreams. He was actually a grown man when teddy bears came into being. Imagine, the most loved toy of all time, and in my lifetime I actually met a man who remembered seeing ads for the newest toy in town, the teddy bear.

I was the fool, you know. I left him with a teddy bear, but I should have gone back to see him again and again. Why, that man had lived a century of life in America. He was born only fifteen years after the Civil War. Ah, the stories he could have told me.

Valentine, you were right about dreams. Life can get in the way. But you might want to know that you really touched my heart, and the bears and I remain dreamers through and through.

I like to think he kept that bear, and that it saw him through to 110. I don't know. Do you ever out grow your need for comfort?

There was once a man named Valentine. He knew a world before teddy bears. And that is hard to imagine.

Chapter 29

Teddy's Legacy

It is hard to believe that a toy patterned after the animals of the woods and zoo and named after a big game-hunting president would be an almost half-a-billion dollar industry at its centennial mark. By the very nature of the soft materials and hand finishing required in making teddy bears, even factory-made bears have unique qualities. No two bears are ever really just alike. Look at a shelf full of the same type of teddy bear and you'll see that each will hold its head a little differently, smile a unique smile and appeal to different individuals.

As for me, I have loved them since I was a child. Teddy bears speak of gentleness, outstretched arms and hearts that understand we are just human—full of frailties and foibles but made of love.

Teddy bears are good for a laugh, too. From Pooh's head stuck in a honey jar to Radar O'Reilly's teddy, the childish antics of bears have been used for comic relief this past hundred years.

When all is said and done, no two bears are the same. It is not only because of the nature of the soft materials from which they are made, but the humans to whom they become attached. There are saggy, old bears that have been loved to softness by a tiny child's hands and there are fine Steiff bears that have spent all their lives on the top shelf. They each have a unique appeal and a story to tell. Teddy bears are about memories and dreams of a world filled with gentle longing, backyard tea parties, and the unconditional love of a friend that knows how to listen, really listen.

When you search for the perfect teddy bear, you may remember the friend and companion of your childhood whose fur was worn thin by kisses. Or you might think of a pristine Steiff bear or a more modern bear that bounces across your mind in soft new colors. Teddy bears are so much a part of childhood in America that few of us can imagine growing up without one and not many grown-ups can resist the appealing glint in a teddy bear's eye and the enduring love in a teddy bear's smile.

When you search for the perfect teddy bear,
you may remember the
friend and companion of your childhood

*The teddy bear, though often relegated to the
nursery floor or an old box in the attic, is ironically,
one of the most beloved symbols of childhood*

In this fast-paced hi-tech world, fads come and go. But the teddy bear remains one of America's all-time, best-loved toys and a constant reminder of a time when life was so very simple.

For me, teddy bear collecting is also about a lifestyle where teddy bears are more than childhood playmates, they are real with lives and possessions all their own. Beautiful old bears and whimsical artist bears have that way of helping this responsible adult reach through the fog of day to day, and find that wonder-filled place of innocence and guilelessness of a child. Bits of old lace, a fainted picture postcard, a love letter from long ago, and the sigh of an old teddy bear take the edge off of a somewhat hard world. Some people run for enjoyment, others climb mountains or fly bright colored kites, but some of us are always in search of that key to the past that roots us in today, and guides us gently into the future.

The teddy bear, though often relegated to the nursery floor or an old box in the attic, is ironically, one of the most beloved symbols of childhood. Baseball cards, apple pie and little red wagons are all images of Americana but none stands above the teddy bear.

In their own way, the Winnie-the-Pooh books explain this attraction to teddy bears. Although Pooh is said to be "a bear of little brain," he seemed to understand what all grown-ups know and Christopher Robin could only guess—sooner or later, the world interferes with childhood. The years and knowledge that come with aging complicates innocence. At the end of House at Pooh Corner, Christopher Robin begins his journey toward knowledge about things like the letter A, about factoring numbers and about kings. He has to leave the forest for school.

Then, suddenly again, Christopher Robin, who was still looking at the world, with his chin in his hands, called out

"Pooh!"
"Yes?" said Pooh.
"When I'm--when------Pooh!"
"Yes, Christopher Robin?"
"I'm not going to do Nothing any more."
"Never again?"
"Well, not so much. They don't let you."

Maybe that is what we see in an old teddy bear—the time in our lives
when the world and obligations didn't rule our days and our minds.
Once you are all grown up you can never really go back.

But childhood,
like the teddy bear and the forest,
lives on forever in your heart.

THE END

TEDDY ROOSEVELT'S
BEAR HUNT

Pres. Theodore Roosevelt came to Smedes, 2 mi. S, in 1902 to hunt. On Nov. 14, Roosevelt refused to shoot a captive bear. Cartoons of the event are thought to have led to the creation of the "Teddy Bear."

The History of the Teddy Bear

Who made the first teddy bear is a subject of many disputes. Some people say the original is German and others are sure that it was made in America. There are many legends about how the teddy bear got its start, but it seems clear that the basic story of the origin of the teddy bear began on that hunting trip to Mississippi. On November 14, 1902 our President, Theodore Roosevelt refused to shoot a tired, tethered little bear which had been offered to him as consolation for a disappointing hunt.

At the very same time that the president was off hunting in Mississippi, two independent entrepreneurs were at work worlds apart. Margarete Steiff was in her workroom in Geingen, Germany creating beautiful stuffed animals, and Rose Michtom and her husband Morris were making handmade candies for their confectioner's shop in Brooklyn. All were unaware that a political cartoon was about to change their lives.

Clifford Berryman, a well-known political cartoonist, immortalized the president's hunt with an illustration of President Roosevelt "drawing the line" in Mississippi. Seems the president said that he could not face his own children if he shot the poor, helpless bruin that had been brought to him. "Drawing the line" was actually a reference to the real reason that Mr. Roosevelt was in the South anyway. He had come to Smedes, Mississippi to settle a border dispute between Mississippi and Louisiana. Although Roosevelt was famous as a big game hunter, by not shooting that helpless bear, the president demonstrated the concern and tender-heartedness for which teddy bears have become known.

Berryman's first cartoon of Theodore Roosevelt and the bear appeared on November 16, 1902. The bear was so popular that Clifford Berryman continued to draw bears in many of his cartoons that featured the president. In the original cartoon the bear was large, and not very appealing, but by the third cartoon the bear had become a cute, wide-eyed bear cub. Before the end of that year, the cub was a familiar character to the Washington Post readership. On December 25, 1902, Berryman drew a cartoon featuring the

little bear himself. Its caption was "Christmas Dreams" and pictured a tiny bruin sitting up in a brass bed in front of the White House. The cub had just awakened from a nightmare featuring a giant bearskin covering one side of the White House.

On inauguration day (March 4, 1905) the Washington Post featured Berryman's cartoon of "Roosevelt's Bear" on page one. The cartoon is drawn like a comic strip in a series of eight boxes. Each section is captioned with a date to tell the story of the evolution of the bear. Berryman always referred to the tiny cub as "Roosevelt's Bear," and legend has it that the president called the cub "Berryman's Bear."

Meanwhile, back to the actual creation of the first toy teddy bear, it really is not clear who made the first teddy bear—Rose Michtom for the window of her Brooklyn candy store or Margaret Steiff of the Steiff factory in Germany. What we do know is that Steiff continues today and is considered to be the ultimate maker of fine teddy bears, and that Rose and Morris were actually able to close the confectionery business on the strength of her teddy bears. The Michtoms were the founders of the Ideal Toy and Novelty Company, later to be known as the Ideal Toy Company. One of those original Ideal bears now lives at the Smithsonian.

History can be confusing. When you are in the middle of the day-to-day, you sometimes forget to write things down or save the letter and documents. Sometimes new ideas seem to float on the air making people even worlds away simultaneously create the same "new" invention. There was supposed to be a letter from Rose to President Roosevelt requesting permission to call their bear "Teddy's Bear." And the Michtom's say that the president responded with a note to the effect that if using his name would help them sell bears and increase business, then they had his blessing—although he could not see how his name would make the difference. Ah, yes, Mr. President, I wonder what this beloved toy would be called if not "Teddy."

Margarete Steiff had been stricken with polio as a child. Undaunted by her paralysis, she studied dressmaking and was the first person in the town of Giengen, Germany, to own a sewing machine. In 1880, Margarete created tiny elephant pincushions as gifts for her nieces and nephews. In 1897, Margarete's nephew Richard joined her company. Richard actually designed the first Steiff bear from a drawing that he had made while visiting a local zoo.

Steiff's early toy bears were articulated in the same way that dolls of the day were jointed, and his bear could be dressed and played with in much the same way as a doll. Margarete, although not totally sold on the concept, agreed to make prototypes for her nephew to take to the Leipzig Trade Fair in 1903. While the bear received a lukewarm reception from most buyers, one enterprising buyer, Hermann Berg, from the Geo. Borgfeldt Company (New York) ordered 3,000 pieces. Steiff company records say that this all happened at the very end of the fair as the Steiffs' were nailing their wooden crates closed.

It seems that Mr. Berg stopped by to complain that he had not seen anything new. Could they design something new for him? It is said that Richard simply walked over to one of the crates and pulled out the bear. The Steiff company's first bear was called Bear 55 PB, and what that means, I have not a clue, but records do show that they registered the design and pattern at the Court in Heidenheim on July 13, 1903.

Does it matter who made the first first teddy bear – Rose and Morris Michtom or Margarete Steiff? The evidence is not totally clear, but the truth is that they each created a toy that is made of pure joy and that remains a century later, to be inseparable from the magic of childhood.

Grand-nephew of Margarete Steiff
Mr. and Mrs. Hans Otto Steiff

Just a couple more, and please write to me.

Before I could get In Search of Teddy to the publisher new teddy bear tales were coming my way. One of my friends, whom I asked to do a final read through of the manuscript, realized that he had a teddy bear story of his own. Kerry Kennedy told me about a bear that had been given to him by his mother. The teddy bear had traveled through life with him, a familiar object, but never as a great comforter. As life would have it just about the time that Kerry read In Search of Teddy his dog Chappy died. Kerry said that he found himself searching out Teddy and just sitting on his sofa thinking about the stories he had just read and receiving real comfort from that old childhood bear.

Then on September 11, 2001, our American way of life changed forever. I was in New York City when the World Trade Centers were hit and collapsed. Something in me said that teddy bears would be pressed into service during the aftermath of that disaster. And they were. A friend told me a wonderful story of school children who wanted to do something for a classroom of their peers. It seems that the boys and girls were from a place far away from the crash site, but television made them so aware of what a terrible thing had happened in the world. So they decided to adopt a class of Brooklyn children and his son's class became the recipients of pre-loved and well-worn teddy bears as a show of concern and comfort. He said that he cried when he saw the bedraggled little character that his son brought home to show him. There is something about the image of a child giving up their much-loved teddy bear to comfort another that says so much about the true art of giving.

The October 12, 2001 edition of USA TODAY reported that thousands of teddy bears showed up, at least one for every seat, at the Central Park memorial service for Cantor Fitzgerald, the company who lost the most employees as a result of the World Trade Center's destruction.

Teddy bears, they can't really change a thing – bring back a lost loved one, turn back the hands of time, but comfort – sometimes all we need is to be comforted and the teddy bear's outstretched arms may be the best we humans have to offer when our grief is beyond words.

I hope we can continue to share our stories, if you have a teddy bear story, would you please write to me?

InSearchofTeddy@aol.com

or
Joan Greene
In Search of Teddy
Hobby House Press
1 Corporate Drive
Grantsville, MD 21536

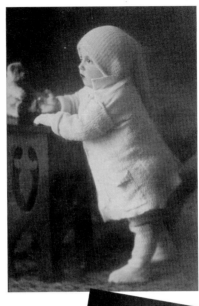

Resources

There is no rhyme or reason to this resource section. I can't promise a wonderful experience at the *Places to Visit* – that is up to you. And if you are buying something, you be the judge. Take care before sending money. I have mostly listed places I have been, organizations that I think are good related to bears, and some basics that you might need if you are a teddy bear lover or if you want to learn more about collecting teddy bears. Because of space constraints, I am sure that I have left out people and places that should be here. The teddy bear magazines are a wealth of information so use what I am giving you as a starting point.

Organizations

Good Bears of the World
P. O. Box 13097
Toledo, OHIO 43613
www.goodbearsoftheworld.org
(See page 109)

World Wildlife Fund Canada
245 Eglinton Ave. East
Suite 410
Toronto, Ontario M4P 3J1
1-866-435-7993
www.wwf.ca
You can adopt a polar bear or a giant panda. Both are on the endangered species list. This makes a great gift for a teddy bear lover.

Teddy Bear Publications

Teddy Bear and Friends Magazine
6405 Flank Drive
Harrisburg, PA 17112
800-829-3340
Teddybearandfriends.com

Teddy Bear Review
P.O. Box 1948
Marion, OH 43305
715-445-5000

Teddy Bear Repair

Be very careful before you have a treasured old friend repaired. As with most antiques less is more and a worn paw simply speaks of years of love. Always call first.

The Teddy Trauma Center
Pat Johnson (A.K.A. Dr. Pat. She has almost twenty years of experience)
2121 Contra Costa Ave.
Santa Rosa, Ca. 95405
707-578-8809

Patterns

Butterick Patterns
Any local fabric store
As of October 2002 find teddy bear patterns inspired by In Search of Teddy by Joan Greene

Places to Visit

The following are places that a teddy bear would visit if they could get a driver's license so don't miss them if you happen to be in the area.

Theodore Roosevelt's Birthplace
28 East 20th Street
New York, NY 10003
212-260-1616
(This site is administered by the National Park Service.)

Pollock's Toy Museum
1 Scala St.
London, England W1P 1LT, UK
011-44-171-636-3452

The Margaret Strong Museum
1 Manhattan Square
Rochester, NY 14607
716-263-2700

Teddy Bear Museum of Naples
2511 Pine Ridge Road
Naples, FL 33942
813-598-9239

Smithsonian Institution
(An original Ideal Toy Company
bear is housed here.)
Washington, D. C.

Winnie-the-Pooh
(See the original Winnie-the-Pooh and his playmates)
Donnell Library Center -- A branch of the New York City Public Library
20 West 53rd Street
New York, NY 10019
212-621-0618

Teddy Bear Shows

Linda Mullins
P. O. Box 2327
Carlsbad, Ca. 92018
760-434-7444
ambssdrbr@aol.com

Teddy Bear Convention
Nevada City, California
P. O. Box 328
Nevada City, Ca. 95959
530-265-5804

ABC Unlimited Productions
632 Pheasant Trail
Frankfort, IL 60423
815-464-3470
teddy@famvid.com

Pat Moore
7022 SE Holgate
Portland, OR 97206
503-775-3324

D. L. Harrison Company, Inc.
303 Deep Dale Court
Timonium, MD 21093
410-252-5192
dlharrison.vista.com

Where to buy antique bears

Barbara Lauver
(I have enjoyed buying several bears from Barbara over the years.)
Harper General Store
10482 Jonestown Road,
Annville, PA 17003
717-865-3456
belauver@desupernet.net

Gigi's Dolls and Sherry's Teddy Bears
(Antique and new dolls and teddy bears)
6029 N. Northwest Hwy.
Chicago, IL 60631
773-594-1540

Collector Clubs

Most companies have collector clubs that you can join for special offerings, newsletters, and such. There is usually a fee to join.

Dean's Collector's Club
Hobby House Press, Inc.
1 Corporate Drive
Grantsville, MD 21536

Japan Teddy Bear Association
Kayoko Jennings
3839 Point of the Rocks Drive
Colorado Springs, CO 80918
JenningsJTBA@aol.com

Merrythought Collector's Club
P. O., Box 577
Oakdale, CA 95361

Steiff Club
Raynham, MA 02768
800-830-0429

Muffy VanderBear® Fan Club
North American Bear Co., Inc.
401 North Wabash, Suite 500
Chicago, IL 60611

Teddy-Hermann Collectors' Club
Postfach 1207
96112 Hirschaid, Germany

Teddy Bear Making Materials and Supplies

Edinburgh Imports, Inc.
P. O. Box 340
Newbury Park, CA 91319
805-376-1700
www. Edinburgh.com

Monterey Mills
1725 E. Delavan Dr.
Janesville, WI 53545
800-432-9959

Teddy Bear Artists
(Again, a great source to find one-of-a-kind artist bears is by going to a teddy bear show or perusing the pages of one of the teddy bear publications.)

Etta Foran
P. O. Box 3731
Joliet, IL 60434

Beverly Port
360-373-0622

Bette Carter
3335 Argyle Drive South
Salem, OR 97302
503-585-2617

Best Chocolate

Teuscher Chocolateir
620 Fifth Ave.
New York, NY
(P.S. Please don't tell my editor about this chocolate thing. This is a teddy bear book, you know. Teuscher has shops here and there, but my favorite is at Rockefeller Center. This is expensive candy; why a teddy bear and a human at tea could eat a hundred dollars worth without blinking.)

Photo Credits

Chuck Atkins: Photographer
Page 70 (1910 Steiff on left and handmade by Joan Greene on right),
Page 95 (1940's British made bear)

Author's Collection of Vintage Photographs
Title page, copyright page, pages 10, 12, 16, 24,32, 33, 38, 42,52, 63,
64,76, 78, 82, 84, 88, 96, 97, 104, 113, 122 (1980's book), 130 (A gift
from the Glenn Sousa Collection), 132, 134, 135, 138, 142, 151,159

Ashton-Drake Galleries (Photography Courtesy of ADG)
Photography by Uldis Saule assisted by Chuck Atkins
Costumes unless noted designed by Joan Greene
Art Direction: Joan Greene
Page 26 (Bear by Pat Joho and Etta Foran),Page 40 (Bear by Brenda
Dewey), Page 46 (Bear by Barbara Sixby), Page 74 (Bear by Barbara Sixby)
Page 98 (Bear by Brenda Dewey), Page 100 (Bears and costumes by Marcia
Sibol), Page 101, Page 106 (Bears by Pat Blair), Page 108 (Bear and Dog
by Pat Joho and Etta Foran), Page 114 (Bear and frog by Etta Foran), Page
152 (Bears by Pat Blair and Iris Cain)

Karen Burnes: Photographer
Page 36

Photographer
Dave Marcus

Courtesy Catherine Bordi
Page 118

Courtesy Gund®
Pages 62 (Snuffles)

Courtesy Michel Durkson Clise from the book, My Circle of Bears
Photography © Marsha Burns
Page 143

Courtesy Viola Russ McBride
Page 72

Courtesy Paul and Rosemary Volpp
Pages 88 and 90 (Bear is called Happy and is a 1926 Steiff)

Etta Foran: Photographer
Page 121,160

Joan Greene: Photographer
Pages 17 (Bear by Hillary Hulen), 18, 20, 28 (Bear designed by Joan
Greene for Hallmark, Inc.), 39, 44, 45,55, 65, 89, 124, 135, 146, 149, 157

Dave Marcus: Photographer
Art Direction: Joan Greene
Page 49 (Bears by Pat Carriker), Page 50 (Bears by Dianne Turborg), Pages 54, 59, 68, 117, 120, 158

Donna Mehalko: Illustrator
Page 145

Michael O'Sullivan: Illustrator
© Bears To Go -- End papers

Roosevelt Bear Books by Seymour Eaton -- Public Domain
pages 58, 79, 126

Uldis Saule: Photogrpaher
Assisted by Chuck Atkins or Jerry Cox
Art Direction: Joan Greene
Cover (Bear is BB bear - author's collection), Dedication page, pages 6, 8,14 (Bear by Etta Foran and Pat Joho and monkey vintage Steiff), 22, 30 (1930's English teddy and in foreground 1906 bear made from a kit), 34, 43 (Bear by Brenda Dewey), 56 (Early Hermann Bear), 60, 66 (BB in back and bear in front by Etta Foran and Pat Joho), 86 (1950'a Panda), Page 102, Page 110 (Bears 1910 Steiff front, American 1930's to left, and early Ideal Bear to right), 136, 140 (Helga and BB, several Schucco Bears, etc.),

Teddy Bears of Whitney, England
Page 92

Just always loved this old photo

About the Author

Joan Greene's heartwarming stories about people and their bears have been giving soul to the teddy bear industry for years. The co-author of The Complete Book of Teddy Bears, Joan first gained national attention as a groundbreaking teddy bear retailer. Her Bears to Go store, specializing in teddy bears, was one of the first of its kind in the United States. Her Bears to Go Wishbook was the first mail-order catalog of handmade artist bears ever published and teddy bear artists world over aspired to have their work featured within its beautiful pages.

An artist herself, Joan has designed and consulted for some of the nation's best-loved collectibles companies from Hallmark Cards, Inc., Butterick Patterns, to Willitts Designs. She started both the Gallery Teddy Bear Division and the Gene Doll Program for Ashton-Drake Galleries.

She currently lives in Chicago with her dog Dottie and more teddy bears than you can count.